THE DEATH PENALTY

POINT/COUNTERPOINT

Philosophers Debate Contemporary Issues
General Editors: James P. Sterba and Rosemarie Tong

This new series provides a philosophical angle to debates currently raging in academic and larger circles. Each book is a short volume (around 200 pages) in which two prominent philosophers debate different sides of an issue. Future topics might include the canon, the ethics of abortion rights, and pornography. For more information contact Professor Sterba, Department of Philosophy, University of Notre Dame, Notre Dame, IN 46566, or Professor Tong, Department of Philosophy, Davidson College, Davidson, NC 28036.

Political Correctness: For and Against
Marilyn Friedman, Washington University, St. Louis
Jan Narveson, University of Waterloo, Ontario, Canada
Humanitarian Intervention: Just War vs. Pacifism
Robert L. Phillips, University of Connecticut
Duane L. Cady, Hamline University
Affirmative Action: Social Justice or Unfair Preference?
Albert G. Mosley, Ohio University
Nicholas Capaldi, University of Tulsa
Religion in the Public Square: The Place of Religious Convictions in Political Debate
Robert Audi, University of Nebraska
Nicholas Wolterstorff, Yale University
Sexual Harassment: A Debate
Linda LeMoncheck
Mane Hajdin, University of Waikato
The Death Penalty: For and Against
Louis P. Pojman, United States Military Academy
Jeffrey Reiman, American University

THE DEATH PENALTY

For and Against

Louis P. Pojman
Jeffrey Reiman

ROWMAN & LITTLEFIELD PUBLISHERS, INC.
Lanham • Boulder • New York • Oxford

ROWMAN & LITTLEFIELD PUBLISHERS, INC.

Published in the United States of America
by Rowman & Littlefield Publishers, Inc.
4720 Boston Way, Lanham, Maryland 20706

12 Hid's Copse Road
Cummor Hill, Oxford OX2 9JJ, England

British Library Cataloguing in Publication Information Available

Library of Congress Cataloging-in-Publication Data
Pojman, Louis P.
 The death penalty : for and against / Louis P. Pojman, Jeffrey
Reiman.
  p. cm.—(Point/counterpoint)
 Includes bibliographical references and index.
 ISBN 0-8476-8632-9 (cloth).—ISBN 0-8476-8633-7 (paper)
 1. Capital punishment. I. Reiman, Jeffrey H. II. Title.
III. Series.
 HV8694.P57 1998
 364.66—dc21   97-27795
                                                           CIP

ISBN 0-8476-8632-9 (cloth : alk. paper)
ISBN 0-8476-8633-7 (pbk. : alk. paper)

Printed in the United States of America

♾ ™ The paper used in this publication meets the minimum requirements of
American National Standard for Information Sciences—Permanence of Paper for
Printed Library Materials, ANSI Z39.48–1984.

Contents

18 98 *

102681

For
Hugo Adam Bedau
and
Ernest van den Haag

Preface and Acknowledgments

Today, in the United States, more than three thousand people are on death row awaiting execution. When Americans are asked in polls whether they favor the death penalty for convicted murderers, they answer overwhelmingly in the affirmative. Asked a more complicated question, such as whether they would favor life in prison without chance of parole over the death penalty, large numbers defect from the death penalty camp in favor of genuine lifetime incarceration—especially if it includes work by convicted murderers aimed at making some restitution to victims' loved ones. Likewise, since the Supreme Court gave the green light to death penalty legislation in 1976, almost every state in the union has passed laws providing capital punishment for specially grave murders. And yet, for all that, few convicted murderers get executed. Prosecutors ask for the death penalty in only a fraction of the cases in which they could, juries approve it in only a fraction of the cases in which it is asked, and a substantial number of death sentences are overturned on appeal. It seems in short that Americans are deeply ambivalent about the death penalty—they believe it's right but they're reluctant to impose it. Though such ambivalence may make life difficult for policy makers, it doesn't necessarily speak badly of Americans. They are, it seems, pulled between the noble desire to do justice and the equally worthy instinct of compassion. They are living out in the "real world" just the sort of moral conflict that philosophers try to clarify and resolve in their world of theories.

It was such a thought that led to the writing of this book. Our aim is not to replace the thinking of American citizens, but to try to identify in their full complexity the fundamental considerations that weigh for and against the death penalty, to argue forcefully on both sides of the issue so that thoughtful persons—students and citizens generally—might make use of the work that philosophers have done on this vexed topic in order to arrive at their own conclusions.

What follows is in the form of a debate: The first essay, arguing for the death penalty, was written by Louis Pojman. The second essay, arguing against the death penalty, was written by Jeffrey Reiman. These are followed by a reply to Reiman's essay by Pojman, and a reply to Pojman's essay by Reiman. Each author wrote a complete draft of his essay before seeing the other's—however, once written, each sent a copy of his essay to the other and received comments and suggestions on it. Likewise with the replies. Thus, while this was a debate, it was not a debate aimed at winning points. Each author freely offered help to the other in making the best argument for his case. And each author heartily thanks the other for that help which both authors believe improved the essays considerably. The authors also suggest that readers read this book in the same spirit in which it was written: look not to win but to figure out where the best arguments lie.

The authors are happy to thank Ernest van den Haag (who discussed this project with Louis Pojman, and who earlier debated the topic—live and in print—with Jeffrey Reiman) and Hugo Adam Bedau (who read and commented on a draft of Jeffrey Reiman's essay) for sharing with us the wisdom that each has accumulated after decades of reflection and writing on this topic. Because of their signal contributions to the philosophical discussion of the moral dimensions of capital punishment, we dedicate this book to them.

We thank as well, Jim Sterba, professor of philosophy at the University of Notre Dame and general editor (with Rosemarie Tong) of the Rowman & Littlefield series "Point/Counterpoint: Philosophers Debate Contemporary Issues," for suggesting this book and inviting the authors to write it. We hope we have lived up to the faith he showed in us. Louis Pojman also expresses his gratitude to John Kleinig, Michael Levin, and Tziporah Kasachkoff for commenting on earlier drafts of his essay. Both authors thank Cindy Nixon for her careful and intelligent editing of the manuscript.

Louis Pojman thanks his wife Trudy, and Jeffrey Reiman thanks his wife Sue Headlee, for all those things that make life and work possible and joyful and for which words are no match.

                                                        L.P. & J.R.

1

For the Death Penalty

Louis P. Pojman

Introduction

What kind and what degree of punishment does public justice take as its principle and norm? None other than the principle of equality in the movement of the pointer of the scale of justice, the principle of not inclining to one side more than to the other. Thus any undeserved evil which you do to someone else among the people is an evil done to yourself. If you rob him, you rob yourself; if you slander him, you slander yourself; if you strike him, you strike yourself; and if you kill him, you kill yourself.

Immanuel Kant.[1]

On August 15, 1990, Angel Diaz, age 19, was sentenced in the Bronx for the murder of an Israeli immigrant who had employed one of Diaz's friends. After strangling the man with a shoelace and stabbing him, Diaz and four friends donned Halloween masks to rob, beat, and gang-rape the man's wife and 16-year-old daughter. The women were then sexually tortured while the murdered man's 3-year-old daughter watched from her crib.

Angel Diaz already had been convicted of burglary four times before he was 16 years old. Diaz's lawyer, Paul Auerbach, said that Diaz was an

---

I wish to thank Ernest van den Haag for helping me get started on this project. Robert Audi, Anthony Hartle, John Kekes, John Kleinig, Michael Levin, Stephen Nathanson, Peter Stromberg, Jeffrey Reiman and Tziporah Kasachkoff made valuable suggestions and criticisms on earlier drafts of this essay.

1. Immanuel Kant, *The Metaphysics of Morals*, trans. E. Hastie (Edinburgh, 1887; originally published 1779), 155.

1

honest boy forced by poverty to do bad things. Diaz was sentenced to prison for 38 and one-third years to life on thirteen counts of murder, robbery, burglary, and conspiracy. His accomplice, Victor Sanchez, 21, who worked for the murdered man and planned the murder, had already been sentenced to 15 years to life.[2]

The National Center of Health Statistics has reported that the homicide rate for young men in the United States is four to seventy-three times the rate of other industrialized countries. In 1994, 23,330 murders were committed in the United States. Whereas killings per 100,000 by men 15 through 24 years old in 1987 was 0.3 in Austria and 0.5 in Japan, the figure was 21.9 in the United States and as high as 232 per 100,000 for blacks in some states. The nearest nation to the United States was Scotland, with a 5.0 homicide rate. In some central city areas the rate is 732 times that of men in Austria. In 1994, the rate was 37 per 100,000 men between the ages of 15 and 24.[3] The number of homicides in New York City broke the 2,000 mark in 1990. Black males in Harlem are said to have a lower life expectancy than males in Bangladesh. Escalating crime has caused an erosion in the quality of urban living. It is threatening the fabric of our social life.

Homo sapiens is the only species in which it is common for one member to kill another. In most species when there is a conflict between individuals, the weaker party submits to the stronger through some ritual gesture and is then permitted to depart in peace. Only in captivity, where the defeated animal cannot get away, will it be killed. Only human beings deliberately kill other individuals and groups of their own species. Perhaps it is not that we are more aggressive than other species but that our drives have been made more lethal by the use of weapons. A weapon, such as a gun or bomb, allows us to harm or kill without actually making physical contact with our victim. A person with a gun need not even touch his or

---

2. "Jail for Crime That Shocked Even the Jaded," *New York Times* (August 16, 1990).

3. Statistics are from the National Center of Health Statistics and are available from the Center for Disease Control. The National Center for Injury Prevention and Control reports that, in 1994, 8,116 young people aged 15 to 24 were victims of homicide. This amounts to an average of 22 youth victims per day in the United States. This homicide rate is 10 times higher than Canada's, 15 times higher than Australia's and 28 times higher than France's and Germany's. In 1994 in the United States 102,220 rapes and 618,950 robberies were reported.

her victim. Someone who sends a letter bomb through the mail may never have even laid eyes on the victim. The inhibition against killing is undermined by the trigger's power, a point to be kept in mind when discussing gun-control legislation. Airplane bomber pilots need not even see their victims as they press the button unleashing destruction. We are a violent race whose power of destruction has increased in proportion to our technology.

Naturally, the subject of punishment should receive increased attention, as should the social causes of crime. As a radical student activist in the 1960s, I once opposed increased police protection for my neighborhood in Morningside Heights, New York City, arguing that we must get to the causes of crime rather than deal only with the symptoms. I later realized that this was like refusing fire fighters the use of water hoses to put out fires because they only dealt with the symptoms rather than the causes of the fire.

The truth is that we do not know the exact nature of what causes crimes of violence. Males commit a disproportionate number of violent crimes in our country, over 90 percent. Why is this? In fact young black males (between the ages of 15 and 24) constitute the group with the greatest tendency towards violent crimes.[4] Many people in the United States believe that *poverty causes crime*, but this is false. Poverty is a terrible condition, and surely contributes to crime, but it is not a necessary or sufficient condition for violent crime. The majority of people in India are far poorer than most of the American poor, yet a person, male or female, can walk through the worst slum of Calcutta or New Delhi at any time of the day or night without fearing molestation. As a student I lived in a very poor neighborhood in a city in England which was safer than the Midwestern middle-class neighborhood in which I grew up. The use and trafficking of illegal drugs contributes to a great deal of crime, and the turn from heroin to crack as the "drug of choice" has exacerbated the matter, but plenty of crime occurred in our society before drugs became the problem they now are. Thus we leave the subject of the causes of crime for psychologists and sociologists to solve and turn to the nature of punishment.

---

4. The United States 1994 *Uniform Crime Report* states that 1,864,168 violent crimes occurred in 1994; 25,052 offenders were listed. "Of those whom sex and age were reported 91% of the offenders were males, and 84% were persons 18 years of age or older. . . . Of offenders for whom race was known, 56% were black, 42% white, and the remainder were persons of other races" (p. 14).

My discussion will be divided into two parts. In Part I, I discuss the major theories of punishment, preparing the way for a discussion of capital punishment. In Part II, I argue that a proper understanding of the nature of punishment justifies capital punishment for some crimes.

Part I: Punishment

To be responsible for a past act is to be liable to praise or blame. If the act was especially good, we go further than praise. We reward it. If it was especially evil, we go further than blame. We punish it. In order to examine the notion of punishment and then that of capital punishment, we first need to inquire under what conditions, if any, criminal punishment is justi-fied. We will look at three approaches to this problem: the retributivist, the utilitarian, and the rehabilitationist.

Even though few of us will ever become criminals or be indicted on criminal charges, most of us feel very strongly about the matter of criminal punishment. Something about crime touches the deepest nerves of our imagination. Take the following situations, which are based on newspaper reports from the mid-1990s:

(1) A drug addict in New York City stabs to death a vibrant, gifted, 22-year-old graduate student who has dedicated her life to helping others.
(2) A sex-pervert lures little children into his home, sexually abuses them, and then kills them. Over twenty bodies are discovered on his property.
(3) A man sends his wife and daughter on an airplane trip, puts a time bomb into their luggage, and takes out a million dollar insurance policy on them. The money will be used to pay off his gambling debts and for prostitutes.
(4) A bomb explodes outside the Alfred P. Murrah Federal Building in Oklahoma City, killing more than 160 people and injuring many others.

What is it within us that rises up in indignation at the thought of these atrocities? What should happen to the criminals in these cases? How can the victims (or their loved ones) ever be compensated for these crimes? We feel conflicting emotional judgments of harsh vengeance toward the criminal and, at the same time, concern that we don't ourselves become violent and irrational in our quest for revenge.

The Definition of Punishment

We may define "punishment," or, more precisely, "institutional or legal punishment," as *an evil inflicted by a person in a position of authority upon another person who is judged to have violated a rule.*[5] It can be analyzed into five concepts:

1. *An evil:* To punish is to inflict harm, unpleasantness, or suffering (not necessarily pain). Regarding this concept, the question is: Under what conditions is it right to cause harm or inflict suffering?
2. *For a violation:* The violation is either a moral or a legal offense. The pertinent questions are: Should we punish everyone who commits a moral offense? Need the offense already have been committed or may we engage in preemptive punishment where we have good evidence that the agent will commit a crime?
3. *Done to the offender:* The offender must be judged or believed to be guilty of a crime. Does this rule out the possibility of punishing innocent people? What should we call the process of "framing" the innocent and "punishing" them?
4. *Carried out by a personal agency.*
5. *Imposed by an authority.*

Let us spend a moment examining each of these points and the questions they raise.

1. Punishment is an evil. It may involve corporal punishment, loss of rights or freedom, or even loss of life. These are things we normally condemn as immoral. How does what is normally considered morally wrong suddenly become morally right? To quote H. L. A. Hart, former Oxford University professor of jurisprudence, What is this "mysterious piece of moral alchemy in which the combination of two evils of moral wickedness and suffering are transmuted into good"?[6] Theories of punishment bear

---

5. In the following analysis I am indebted to Anthony Flew, "Justification of Punishment," *Philosophy* (1954); Joel Feinberg, "Punishment," *Philosophy of Law*, 2nd ed., eds. Joel Feinberg and Hyman Gross (Wadsworth, 1980); and Herbert Morris, "Persons and Punishment," *The Monist* 52 (October 1968). See also Tziporah Kasachkoff, "The Criteria of Punishment: Some Neglected Considerations," *Canadian Journal of Philosophy* 2, no. 3 (March 1973).

6. H. L. A. Hart, *Punishment and Responsibility* (Oxford University Press, 1968), 234.

the burden of proof to justify why punishment is required. The three classical theories have been retribution, deterrence, and rehabilitation (or reform of the criminal). We shall examine each of these below. These theories attempt not only to justify types of punishment, but also to provide guidance on the degrees of punishment to be given for various crimes and persons.

2. Punishment is given for an offense, but must it be for a violation of a legal statute or may it also be for any moral failure? While most legal scholars agree that the law should have a moral basis, it is impractical to make laws against every moral wrong. If we had a law against lying, for example, our courts would be cluttered beyond our ability. Also some laws may be immoral (e.g., anti-abortionists believe that the laws permitting abortion are immoral), but they still are laws, carrying with them coercive measures.

Whether we should punish only offenses already committed or also crimes that are intended is a difficult question. If I know or have good evidence that Smith is about to kill some innocent child (but not which one), and the only way to prevent this is by incarcerating Smith (or killing him), why isn't this morally acceptable? Normally, we don't have certainty about people's intentions, so we can't be certain that Smith really means to kill the child. But what if we do have strong evidence in this case? Nations sometimes launch preemptive strikes when they have strong evidence of an impending attack (e.g., Israel in the Six-Day War in 1967 acted on reliable information that Arab nations were going to attack it. It launched a preemptive strike that probably saved many Israeli lives). Although preemptive strikes are about defense, not punishment per se, could the analogy carry over? After all, part of the role of punishment is defense against future crimes.

This is a difficult subject, and I can conceive of conditions under which we would incapacitate would-be criminals before they commit their crimes, but the opportunity for abuse is so enormous here that one needs to tread carefully. In general our laws permit punishing only the guilty, relying on the principle that every dog may have its first bite—or, at least, an attempt at a first bite.

3. Punishment is done to the offender. No criminologist justifies punishing the innocent, but classic cases of framing the innocent in order to maximize utility exist. Sometimes Caiaphus's decision to frame and execute Jesus of Nazareth (John 10:50) is cited. "It were better that one man

should die for a nation than that the whole nation perish." Utilitarians seem to be vulnerable to such practices, but every utilitarian philosopher of law eschews such egregious miscarriages of justice. Why this is so is a point I will discuss below.

This stipulation, "done to an offender," also rules out other uses of the word "punish," as when, for instance, we say that boxer Mike Tyson "punished" his opponent with a devastating left to the jaw. Such metaphorical or non-legal uses of the term are excluded from our analysis. Similarly, we quarantine confirmed or potential disease carriers, but we would not call this imposed suffering "punishment," for our intention is not to cause suffering (but to prevent it) and the carrier is innocent of any wrongdoing.

4. Punishment is carried out by a Personal agency. Punishment is not the work of natural forces but of people. Lightning may strike and kill a criminal, but only people (or conscious beings) can punish other people.

5. Punishment is imposed by an Authority. Punishment is conferred through institutions which have to do with maintaining laws or social codes. This rules out vigilante executions as punishments. Only a recognized authority, such as the state, can carry out legal punishment for criminal behavior.

We turn now to the leading theories on punishment.

Theories of Punishment

Retributivist Theories

Retributivist theories make infliction of punishment dependent upon what the agent, as a wrong-doer, deserves, rather than on any future social utility which might result from the infliction of suffering on the criminal. That is, rather than focusing on any *future* good that might result from punishment, retributivist theories are *backward* looking, assessing the nature of the misdeed. The most forceful proponents of this view are Immanuel Kant (1724–1804), C. S. Lewis (1898–1963), and Herbert Morris. Here is a classic quotation from Kant, which deserves to be quoted at length:

> Juridical punishment can never be administered merely as a means for promoting another good either with regard to the criminal himself or to civil

society, but must in all cases be imposed only because the individual on whom it is inflicted *has committed a crime*. For one man ought never to be dealt with merely as a means subservient to the purpose of another, nor be mixed up with the subjects of real right. Against such treatment his inborn personality has a right to protect him, even though he may be condemned to lose his civil personality. He must first be found guilty and *punishable* before there can be any thought of drawing from his punishment any benefit for himself or his fellow-citizens.

The principle of punishment is a categorical imperative, and woe to him who creeps through the serpent-windings of utilitarianism to discover some advantage that may discharge him from the justice of punishment, or even reduces its amount by the advantage it promises, in accordance with the Pharisaical maxim, "It is better for *one* man to die than for an entire people to perish" [John 10:51]. For if justice and righteousness perish, there is no longer any value in men's living on the earth.

But what kind and what amount of punishment is it that public justice makes its principle and standard? It is the principle of equality, by which the pointer of the scale of justice is made to incline no more to the one side than the other. It may be rendered by saying that the undeserved evil which any one commits on another, is to be regarded as perpetrated on himself. Hence it may be said, "If you slander another, you slander yourself; if you steal from another you steal from yourself; if you strike another, you strike yourself; if you kill another, you kill yourself." This is the *law of retribution (jus talionis)*—it being understood, of course, that this is applied by a court as distinguished from private judgment. It is the only principle that can definitely assign both the quality and the quantity of a just penalty. All other standards are wavering and uncertain; and on account of other considerations involved in them, they contain no principle conformable to the sentence of pure and strict justice.

But what does it mean to say, If you steal from someone, you steal from yourself? Whoever steals makes the property of everyone else insecure and therefore deprives himself (by the principle of retribution) of security in any possible property. He has nothing and can also acquire nothing; but he still wants to live, and this is now possible if others provide for him. But since the state will not provide for him free of charge, he must let it have his powers for any kind of work it pleases (in convict or prison labor) and is reduced to the status of a slave for a certain time, or permanently if the state sees fit. If, however, he has committed murder he must *die*. Here there is no substitute that will satisfy justice. There is no similarity between life, however wretched it may be, and death, hence no likeness between the crime and the retribution unless death is judicially carried out upon the wrongdoer, although it must still be freed from any mistreatment that could make the humanity in the person suffering it into something abominable. Even if a civil society resolved to dissolve itself with the consent of all its members—as might be supposed in the case of a people inhabiting an island resolving to separate and scatter themselves throughout the whole world—the last murderer lying in prison ought to be executed before the resolution was carried out. This ought to be done in order that every one may realize the desert of his deeds, and that bloodguiltiness may not remain upon the people; for otherwise they will all be regarded as participators in the murder as a public violation of justice.[7]

This is a classic expression of the retributivist position, for it bases punishment solely on the issue of whether or not the subject in question has committed a crime and punishes him accordingly. All other considerations—eudaimonistic or utilitarian—are to be rejected as irrelevant to punishment. For example, Kant considers the possibility of a capital criminal allowing himself to be a subject in a medical experiment as a substitute for capital punishment in order to benefit the society. He rejects the suggestion. "A court would reject with contempt such a proposal from a medical college, for justice ceases to be justice if it can be bought for any price whatsoever." I have heard the phrase "that bloodguiltiness may not remain upon the people" interpreted as implying utilitarian consideration, signifying that the people will be cursed in the future. Perhaps a more charitable interpretation is that failure to punish constitutes an endorsement of the criminal act and thus a kind of criminal complicity after the act.[8]

Kant and the classic retributivist position in general have three theses about the justification of punishment:

1. Guilt is a necessary condition for judicial punishment; that is, *only* the guilty may be punished.
2. Guilt is a sufficient condition for judicial punishment; that is, *all* the guilty must be punished. If you have committed a crime, morality demands that you suffer an evil for it.
3. The correct amount of punishment imposed upon the morally (or legally) guilty offender is that amount which is *equal* to the moral seriousness of the offense.

There are various ways of arguing for these theses. One is to argue, as Kant does, that in lying, stealing, unjustly striking, or killing another, the

---

7. Immanuel Kant, *The Metaphysics of Morals* (1779), trans. E. Hastie (Edinburgh, 1887), 155–56.
8. I am grateful to Jeffrey Reiman for pointing this out to me.

offender lies, steals, unjustly strikes or kills himself. That is, by universalizing the maxim of such acts, the offender wills a like action on himself. This is the law of retaliation (*jus talionis*). "The undeserved evil which anyone commits on another is to be regarded as perpetuated on himself." The criminal need not consciously desire the same punishment, but by acting on such a principle, for example, "murder your enemies," the offender implicitly draws the same treatment on himself. He deserves to suffer in the same way he has harmed another. Or, at least, the suffering should be equal and similar to the suffering he has caused. This is the *strict equality* (sometimes called the *"lex talionis"*) interpretation of retributivism.

The weakness of the equality interpretation is that it is both impractical and impossible to inflict the very same kind of suffering on the offender as he has imposed on others. Our social institutions are not equipped to measure the exact amount of harm done by offenders or repay them in kind. We rightly shrink from torturing the torturer or resuscitating the serial murderer so that we can "kill" him a second, a third, a fourth time, and so forth. How do you give a trusted member of the FBI or CIA who betrays his country by spying for the enemy an equivalent harm? Our legal systems are not equipped to punish according to the harm inflicted but, rather, according to the wrong done, measured against specified statutes with prescribed penalties.

A second way, following Herbert Morris and Michael Davis, is to interpret these theses in terms of social equilibrium.[9] The criminal has violated a mutually beneficial scheme of social cooperation, thereby treating law-abiding members of the community unfairly. Punishment restores the scales of justice, the social equilibrium of benefits and burdens. We might put the argument this way.

1. In breaking a primary rule of society, a person obtains an unfair advantage over others.
2. Unfair advantages ought to be redressed by society if possible.
3. Punishment is a form of redressing the unfair advantage.
4. Therefore, we ought to punish the offender for breaking the primary rule.

---

9. Herbert Morris, "Persons and Punishment." See also Michael Davis, "Harm and Retribution," *Philosophy & Public Affairs* 15, no. 3 (Summer 1986).

Punishment restores the social equilibrium of burdens and benefits by taking from the agent what he or she unfairly got and now owes, that is, exacting his or her debt. This argument, like the Kantian one above, holds that society has a duty to punish the offender, since society has a general duty to redress "unfair advantages if possible." That is, we have a prima facie duty to eliminate unfair advantages in society, even though that duty may be overridden by other considerations such as the high cost (financially or socially) of doing so or the criminal's repentance.

While the Kantian interpretation focuses on the nature and gravity of the harm done by the offender, Morris's *Unfair Advantage* or *Fair Play Argument* focuses on the unfairness of the offense—the idea of unfair advantage which ought to be repaid to society. Although it is not always the case that the criminal gains an advantage or profit in crime, he or she does abandon the common burden of self-restraint in order to obtain criminal ends. While the rest of us are forgoing the use of unlawful and immoral means to obtain our goals, while we are restraining ourselves from taking these shortcuts, the criminal makes use of these means to his or her ends. As such we have been unfairly taken advantage of, and justice requires the annulment of the unfair advantage. The criminal must repay his or her debt to society. He or she need not be punished in the same way as his or her offense, but the punishment must "fit the crime," be a proportionate response.

It is not clear, however, that Morris's and Davis's interpretation can do all the work. For one thing it is modeled on the act of stealing (or cheating), getting an unfair advantage over others. The criminal may obtain an unfair advantage over others by cheating on exams or taxes, by killing a rival for a job, or by stealing another's purse, but this model of unfair advantage doesn't work as well with sadistic crimes which may leave the criminal psychologically worse off than the victim. The successful rapist may be worse off, not better off, than before his crime. The terrorist who detonates a bomb on the crowded bus he is riding doesn't gain any advantage over others, for he no longer exists. Furthermore, we do not punish all instances of unfair advantage, as when someone lies. Daniel Farrell has objected to the Fair Play Argument, pointing out that even before we enter into a social contract, even in a Lockean state of nature, the concept of just desert holds, and we should intervene on behalf of an innocent victim who is being attacked by an aggressor, a malicious rapist or a killer.[10] Moreover, we think someone is deserving of punishment even when he only *attempts*—with malice aforethought—to harm others, when his intention to do evil is unsuccessful. This is sometimes referred to as *mens rea:* having a guilty mind.

Desert

Both the *Strict Equality* (*lex talionis*) and the *Fair Play* interpretations of retributivism have some validity, but both partially misfire. Strict Equality of punishment is not practical or necessary for retributive justice. On the other hand, the Fair Play argument overemphasizes the advantage gained by the criminal and fails to account for evil intentions, *mens rea*. But both theories correctly point to the broader, underlying ground for punishment: that the criminal deserves suffering in a way fitting his or her crime. Farrell correctly points to this salient feature—*desert*, which exists even in a Lockean state of nature (a precontractual state). While it is not practical, let alone necessary, to punish the criminal in a manner equal to the gravity of the crime, we can punish him or her in a manner proportionate to the seriousness of the offense. So we should modify the third premise of the Strict Equality interpretation to read:

3. The correct amount of punishment imposed upon the morally (or legally) guilty offender is that amount which is proportionate to the moral seriousness of the offense.

The concept of desert has been attacked or, more accurately, downplayed and ignored. John Rawls has asserted that there is no natural desert (for our relative superiority in talents—even the ability to make an effort is a product of heredity and family background). Since we do not deserve our natural endowments and families, we do not deserve what these things produce, our good or bad deeds.[11] Stanley Benn and R. S. Peters have denied any legitimacy to the claims that the virtuous deserve to prosper and the guilty deserve to suffer (let alone that they deserve to suffer in proportion to the gravity of their offenses). They write, "The utilitarian

---

10. Daniel Farrell, "Justification of General Deterrence," *Philosophical Review* XCIV, no. 3 (July 1985).

11. John Rawls, *A Theory of Justice* (Cambridge: Harvard University Press, 1971), 74, 100–105.

can only point out . . . that a great many people think that punishment requires some justification . . . and that though it is intolerable that there should be murder, rape, and dope-peddling, punishment is just one way of reducing the incidence of such admitted evils. He sees nothing intrinsically fitting about this particular way, which itself involves increasing the misery in the world."[12] Robert Goodin holds that *need* overrides desert in a theory of justice. He asks us to suppose that two men have been in an automobile accident and have the same serious injury, but one is guilty of the gross recklessness that caused the accident, while the other is an innocent victim. Who should get priority treatment in the emergency room? Goodin asserts that even if everyone has clear knowledge of the facts, it would be outrageous to give preferential treatment to the innocent victim.[13]

I think that desert deserves a better defense.

The concept of desert is connected with our notion of responsibility. As free agents who can choose, a moral universe would be so arranged that we would be rewarded or punished in a manner equal to our virtue or vice. As the ancient adage puts it, "Whatsoever a man sows that shall he also reap." Those who sow good deeds would reap good results, and those who choose to sow their wild oats would reap accordingly. Given a notion of objective morality, the good should prosper and the evil should suffer— both in equal measure to their virtue or vice. This idea is reflected in the Eastern idea of karma: You will be repaid in the next life for what you did in this one. The ancient Greek philosophers and the Roman jurists, beginning with Cicero, define justice as giving to each his due, *suum cuique tribuens.* Jesus may be seen as adumbrating the same principle in his statement, "Render unto Caesar that which is Caesar's and unto God that which is God's" (Luke 20:25). In the Christian tradition it is reflected in the doctrine of heaven and hell (and purgatory). The good will be rewarded according to their good works and the evil will be punished in hell—which they have chosen by their actions. Leibniz put the matter thusly:

> Thus it is that the pains of the damned continue, even when they no longer serve to turn them away from evil, and that likewise the rewards of the blessed

---

12. Stanley Benn and R. S. Peters, "The Utilitarian Case for Deterrence," in *Contemporary Punishment,* eds. Rudolph Gerber and Patrick McAnany (University of Notre Dame Press, 1972), 97–98.

13. Robert Goodin, "Negating Positive Desert Claims," *Political Theory* 13, no. 4 (November 1985): 574–98.

continue, even when they no longer serve for strengthening them in good. One may say nevertheless that the damned ever bring upon themselves new pains through new sins, and that the blessed ever bring upon themselves new joys by new progress in goodness: for both are founded on the *principle of the fitness of things*, which has seen to it that affairs were so ordered that the evil action must bring upon itself chastisement.[14]

It would seem that eternal hell is excessive punishment for human evil and eternal bliss excessive reward, but the basic idea of *moral fittingness* seems to make sense. Leibniz is referring to the same principle which Kant, as noted above, calls the principle of *equality*, a sort of symmetry between input and output in any endeavor. We get a hint of this symmetry in the practice of gratitude. We normally and spontaneously feel grateful for services rendered. Someone treats us to dinner, gives us a present, teaches us a skill, rescues us from a potential disaster or simply gives us directions. A sense of gratitude wells up inside of us toward our benefactor. We feel indebted, a sense of obligation toward him or her. We sense we have a duty to reciprocate in kind. On the other hand, if someone intentionally and cruelly hurts us, deceives us, betrays our trust, we feel involuntary resentment. We want to reciprocate and harm that person. The offender deserves to be harmed, and we have a right to harm him. If he has harmed someone else, we have an instinctual duty to harm him. Henry Sidgwick argued that these basic emotions are in fact the grounds for our notion of desert: Punishment is resentment universalized and rewards—a sort of positive retribution—gratitude universalized.[15] Whether such a reduction of desert to resentment and gratitude completely explains our notion of desert may be questioned, but it lends support to two theses: first, that there is natural, pre-institutional desert and, second, that desert creates obligations.

John Rawls has influenced a number of social and political thinkers with his suggestion that natural desert does not exist; rather, desert originates a contractual situation (for Rawls, behind the veil of ignorance), where parties to the contract consider fair practices. Desert must be tied to institutions, which may decide to reward and punish in ways that are based on basic principles. But this idea seems to put the cart before the horse.

---

14. G. W. Leibniz, *Theodicy* (trans. E. M. Huggard), 1698.
15. Henry Sidgwick, *Methods of Ethics* (Hackett Publishing Company), bk. III, chap. 5.

Rather than society inventing desert, desert grounds a just society. It is the measure of whether a society is just or unjust. Desert is not invented by society but discovered as a moral requirement, without which the society itself lacks justification.

These reactions of gratitude and resentment are primitive and natural. They are seen in animal behavior as well as in the most primitive human societies. The chimpanzee who is groomed by another chimpanzee will come to the aid of his benefactor. Wolves will kill unreliable members of their pack, who threaten their well-being. Rather than detractors from justice, these primordial reactions may be the grounds of justice, an Ur-justice.

This primordial desert-based idea of justice has two parts: Every action in the universe has a fitting response in terms of creating a duty to punish or reward, and that response must be *appropriate* in measure to the original action. It follows that evil deeds must be followed by evil outcomes and good deeds by good outcomes, exactly equal or in proportion to the vice or virtue in question. That is the basis of a primordial meritocracy, recognized in all cultures and religions but denied or undermined by much of contemporary political philosophy.

I cannot prove this principle to you. It is a basic principle, more certain to me than any of the proofs that would support it. I can only ask you to reflect on the nature of desert and determine whether you see it the same way. If you agree that people deserve the results of their voluntary deeds, then do we not have an obligation to enable them to receive their deserts? Consider this situation: Jane is a devoted wife who puts her husband Jack through medical school, working long hours and sacrificing her education for him. Jack is so fully caught up in his medical studies that he fails to be grateful to Jane for all she is doing. Upon graduating with his M.D., with a lucrative practice in hand, Jack announces to Jane that he has found a younger woman and will be divorcing her. Doesn't Jane deserve an ample alimony, and doesn't Jack deserve not only our censure, but also to have some of his earnings transferred to Jane? Doesn't Jane have a moral claim on Jack which society in general should help enforce?

Or consider two equally talented young adults, Bob and Bill. Bob is a lazy scoundrel. He cheated his way through school, sponges off his friends without feeling the least gratitude, spends his time surfing off the Santa Monica coast, and makes no positive contribution to his community. Bill, on the other hand, not only studied hard for his college degree, but spent his weekends helping to educate poor children. He has lived an exemplary moral life, striving to contribute to the welfare of his community. Through no fault of his own, he has been laid off by a large company that is downsizing. Both Bob and Bill are now in need of your financial help, but you have the means to help only one of them. Who should you help? Doesn't Bill have a general claim to society's help? Doesn't his deserving good create an obligation on us to help him? The obligation is overridden if we lack the resources to help Bill or if we have other duties that take precedence over this one. Bob doesn't deserve our help, but if we have additional resources, we might, nevertheless, choose to help him—hoping to reform him. Our duty to give Bob what he deserves may be overridden by mercy or utility (e.g., we think Bob could make a great surfing instructor for children). But if our best judgment convinces us that Bob will not reform, we may choose to give him what he deserves, which is no help at all.

The same notion of desert-as-creating-obligations underlies our revulsion against prejudicial discrimination. We object to racist and sexist practices because they treat people unfairly: they make irrelevant features, such as race and gender, rather than desert or merit, the criteria for social goods. We have a duty not to harm people unjustly (i.e., not to inflict undeserved harm on them), but we treat them positively according to their moral dignity. Similarly, children who have been afflicted with life-threatening diseases deserve to be compensated by society so that their undeserved suffering is mitigated. Such desert claims create prima facie obligations on all of us who have the means to aid them. This principle seems to be one that is intuitively recognized by people everywhere in their everyday practices. The sociologist George Caspar Homans has noted that in economic relations people in every culture "are alike in holding the notion of proportionality between investment and profit that lies at the heart of distributive justice" and have a notion that "fair exchange . . . is realized when the profit, or reward less cost, of each man is directly proportional to his investment."[16]

Desert and Utilitarianism

One can partially explain our belief in the propriety of rewarding and punishing people according to the nature of their acts by utilitarian consid-

---

16. George Caspar Homans, *Social Behavior: Its Elementary Forms* (Routledge & Kegan Paul, 1961), 246, 264.

erations. Rewarding good works encourages further good works, while punishment has a deterrent effect. By recognizing and rewarding merit, we promote efficiency and welfare. We want the very best generals to lead our sons and daughters to battle, the most outstanding basketball and football players to play on our team, and excellent surgeons, airline pilots, and judges to serve our needs. A superior teacher can teach twice or thrice as effectively as a minimally competent one. We want the best car for our money, not just an average car. While some tasks have thresholds beyond which it is not necessary to improve on (e.g., I'm satisfied with our slow mail delivery, though getting the mail a few hours earlier would be better), some tasks—those mentioned above—crucially depend upon high efficiency. So a utilitarian defense of general meritocracy is possible. In general we can say that a society that has a fitting notion of rewarding those who contribute to its well-being and punishing those who work against its well-being will survive and prosper better than a society lacking these practices. But, of course, utilitarian considerations can be used to override considerations of merit.

Utilitarian considerations are important, but I doubt that they are the whole story behind the long-standing, universal history of our faith in meritocracy. One would like to have a non-utilitarian, *deontological* argument to ground our intuitions that regarding any good and useful function X, the good (at X) should prosper and the bad (at X) should suffer. W. D. Ross argues that meritocracy is a fundamental intuition, offering, as evidence for this thesis, the following thought experiment. After identifying two intrinsically good things (1) pleasure and (2) virtue, Ross asks us to consider a third:

> If we compare two imaginary states of the universe, alike in the total amounts of virtue and vice and of pleasure and pain present in the two, but in one of which the virtuous were all happy and the vicious miserable, while in the other the virtuous were miserable and the vicious happy, very few people would hesitate to say that the first was a much better state of the universe than the second. It would seem then that, besides virtue and pleasure, we must recognize (3), as a third independent good, the apportionment of pleasure and pain to the virtuous and the vicious respectively. And it is on the recognition of this as a separate good that the recognition of the duty of justice, in distinction from fidelity to promise on the one hand and from beneficence on the other, rests.[17]

---

17. W. D. Ross, *The Right and the Good* (Oxford University Press, 1930), 138.

I think that most people would agree with Ross that it is intuitively obvious that the appropriate distribution of happiness and unhappiness should be according to virtue and vice. Even if we could produce more aggregate happiness or welfare by making the vicious better off, would we not prefer a world where people get what they deserve to one of utility? Part of what makes the world good consists in giving people what they deserve. It seems to be exactly the intuition that motivated Kant's dictum that conscientiousness or the good will, being the single desert base, is the only moral basis for happiness: "An impartial spectator can never feel approval in contemplating the uninterrupted prosperity of a being graced by no touch of a pure and good will, and that consequently a good will seems to constitute the indispensable condition of our very worthiness to be happy."[18]

Consider again Farrell's example concerning an aggressor who is attacking an innocent victim in the state of nature. Would we not intervene on behalf of the victim if we thought we could safely make a difference in the outcome? Would we not think it better that the aggressor die than that the victim die? And if two aggressors attacked one victim, so that twice as many *dolors* (units of suffering) were incurred by killing both aggressors in saving the life of the innocent party, would we not prefer this than that the victim die (with the result that half as many dolors resulted)? If the correct answer to these questions is "yes," then not only is desert preinstitutional (contra Rawls and company), but it is a valid concept apart from utilitarian outcomes. If this is so, desert trumps utility.

It also trumps equality. What we object to in inequalities, I think, is that they so often are undeserved. We don't morally object when the better quarterback is chosen as a starter over ourselves, or when a superior student, who works equally hard, gets a higher grade than ourselves, or when an enterprising entrepreneur succeeds in establishing a socially useful business and thereby makes more money than his lazy brother who spends his days surfing off the California coast. What we may object to is the lazy brother inheriting vast sums of money from his enterprising brother, and what we certainly do object to is the lazy brother stealing the money from his brother, for the lazy surfer doesn't deserve his gains.

---

18. Immanuel Kant, *Groundwork of the Metaphysic of Morals*, trans. H. J. Paton (Hutchinson University Library, 1948), 59. For a fuller defense of the thesis that desert creates obligations see my "Merit: Why Do We Value It?" (forthcoming in *Journal of Social Philosophy*).

In sum, our concept of justice includes notions of responsibility, reciprocity, and desert that are preinstitutional and deontological, so that perpetrators of evil deserve to suffer and virtuous people deserve a level of well-being corresponding to their virtue. Since we have a general duty to strive to bring about justice in the world, it follows that we have a duty to try to bring it about directly or indirectly, through just institutions, by which, wherever possible, the virtuous are rewarded with well-being and the vicious with suffering, inclining them to repentance.

This is not to argue that we must always give people what they deserve. There may be grounds for mercy, forgiveness, and rehabilitation: mitigating circumstances may be taken into consideration to lessen the severity of the punishment. But the aim is to bring about moral homeostasis, a social order where the good are rewarded and the bad are punished in proportion to their deeds.

Although we have indirectly addressed it, let us say a word about the third thesis of retribution, stated earlier:

3. The correct amount of punishment imposed upon the morally (or legally) guilty offender is that amount which is proportionate to the moral seriousness of the offense.

The *lex talionis*—"an eye for an eye, a tooth for a tooth, a life for a life" (Exod. 21) set forth by Moses in the Old Testament—was actually a gesture of restraint on the passion for vengeance: A life for an eye or a tooth, two lives for the life of one member of my family. Thomas Jefferson was one of the earliest Americans to set forth a system of proportionality of punishment to crime:

> Whosoever shall be guilty of rape, polygamy, sodomy with man or woman, shall be punished, if a man, by castration, if a woman by cutting through the cartilage of her nose a hole of one half inch in diameter at the least. [And] whosoever shall maim another, or shall disfigure him . . . shall be maimed, or disfigured in the like sort: or if that cannot be, for want of some part, then as nearly as may be, in some other part of at least equal value.[19]

---

19. Thomas Jefferson, *Bill for Proportioning Crime and Punishments* (1779) quoted in Ernest van den Haag, *Punishing Criminals: Concerning a Very Old and Painful Question* (Basic Books, 1975), 193.

This attempt at proportionality seems to be universal. As Émile Durkheim noted, "There is no society where the rule does not exist that the punishment must be proportioned to the offense."[20] We have a general idea of *ordinal* orderings of general crimes according to their gravity, for example (1) murder; (2) rape; (3) theft; (4) perjury—but it is difficult, if not impossible, to give them absolute rankings: for example, "Theft must always be visited with 1 year in prison; burglary, with breaking and entering, with 5 years; perjury with six months," and so on, for it is hard to compare crimes. How much worse is rape than assault? Well, different rapes are of different magnitudes of severity, and likewise with assaults and murders and perjuries and so forth. Some relativity applies to our perceptions of the seriousness of crimes, so that if legal punishment is perceived as excessive, juries will fail to convict; and if legal punishment is perceived as being too lenient, private vengeance will emerge. In either case, the law is subverted. So even if it were the case that rapists deserved castration (as Jefferson advocated) or being raped themselves, if the public perception is that these punishments are too brutal, then the penal system is forced to impose lesser or, at least, different punishments. Complete punitive justice, even if we knew what it was, may not be possible in an imperfect world.

None of this is meant to deny in the least the general thesis that the punishment should fit the crime, that the criminal deserves punishment commensurate to the gravity of the crime. The discussion is meant to urge caution, restraint, a sense of our fallibility, and a realization that an insistence on perfect justice is counterproductive (*summum justicia, summa injuria*—the demand for nothing less than *perfect* justice results in perfect injury). On the other hand, we must seek to respect the demands of impartial justice, inflicting punishments that correspond to the gravity of the crime. Someone who takes another's life in cold blood (*mens rea*), deserves to die, someone who maliciously blinds another deserves blindness or something equivalent, someone who steals from another deserves to lose his possessions or—if he has gambled or spent them—to be punished in a manner deemed suitable by the judicial system (say, a certain length in prison). Roughly equivalent punishments satisfy the notion of symmetry or fittingness inherent in our notion of desert. But not all crimes (e.g., embezzlement and perjury) lend themselves to this symmetry model.

---

20. Émile Durkheim, *The Rules of Sociological Method*, (Oxford University Press, 1952) quoted in van den Haag, *Punishing Criminals*, 194.

There practical wisdom, what the Greeks called *phronesis* is needed. A uniform schedule of penalties for various crimes attempts to provide standardized punishments, removing arbitrariness from the penal system; but the weakness of this system is that it also removes discretion, *phronesis*, from the sentencing process.

Finally, we must separate retributivism from vengeance. Vengeance signifies acts that arise out of the victims' desire for revenge, for satisfying their anger at the criminal for what he or she has done. The nineteenth-century British philosopher James Fitzjames Stephen thought this was a justification for punishment, arguing that punishment should be inflicted "for the sake of gratifying the feeling of hatred—call it revenge, resentment, or what you will—which the contemplation of such [offensive] conduct excites in healthily constituted minds."[21] But retributivism is not based on hatred for the criminal (though a feeling of vengeance may accompany the punishment). Retributivism is the theory that the criminal *deserves* to be punished and deserves to be punished in proportion to the gravity of his or her crime—whether or not the victim or anyone else desires it. We may all deeply regret having to carry out the punishment.

On the other hand, people do have a sense of outrage and passion for revenge at criminals for their crimes. Stephen was correct in asserting that "[t]he criminal law stands to the passion for revenge in much the same relation as marriage to the sexual appetite."[22] Failure to punish would no more lessen our sense of vengeance than the elimination of marriage would lessen our sexual appetite. When a society fails to punish criminals in a way thought to be proportionate to the gravity of the crime, the public is likely to take the law into its own hands, resulting in vigilante justice, lynch mobs, and private acts of retribution. The outcome is likely to be an anarchistic, insecure state of injustice.

Although the retributivist theory has broad intuitive appeal, it is not without problems. One problem is to make sense out of the notion of balancing the scales of justice. The metaphor suggests a cosmic scale which is put out of balance by a crime, but such a scale might not exist, or if one does, it may not be our duty to maintain it through punishment. That may

---

21. Sir James Fitzjames Stephen, *Liberty, Equality, Fraternity* (Cambridge University Press, 1867), 152.

22. Sir James Fitzjames Stephen, *A History of Criminal Law in England* (Macmillan, 1863), 80.

be God's role. Furthermore, retributivism seems unduly retrospective. If we can restore the repentant criminal to moral integrity through rehabilitative processes, then to insist on a pound of flesh seems barbaric. Nevertheless, although retributivism needs to be supplemented by other considerations, it still provides the core idea of justice as distribution on the basis of desert. It will be the basis of my defense of capital punishment in the next part of this work.

Utilitarian Theories

Utilitarian theories are theories of deterrence, reform, and prevention. The emphasis is not on the gravity of the evil done, but on deterring and preventing future evil. Their motto might be, "Don't cry over spilt milk!" Unlike retributive theories which are backward-looking and based on *desert*, Utilitarian theories are *forward*-looking, based on social improvement. Jeremy Bentham (1748–1832) and John Stuart Mill (1806–1873) are classic Utilitarians. Their position can be analyzed into three theses:

1. Social utility (including reform, prevention, and deterrence) is a necessary condition for judicial punishment.
2. Social utility is a sufficient condition for judicial punishment.
3. The proper amount of punishment to be imposed upon the offender is that amount which will do the most good (or least harm) to all those who will be affected by it.

Stanley Benn puts it well: "The margin of increment of harm inflicted on the offender should be preferable to the harm avoided by fixing that penalty rather than one slightly lower."[23]

Punishment is a technique of social control, justified so long as it prevents more evil than it produces. If there is a system of social control that will give a greater balance (e.g., rehabilitation), then the utilitarian will opt for that. The utilitarian doesn't accept Draconian laws that would deter because the punishment would be worse than the crime, causing greater suffering than the original offense. Only three grounds are permissible for punishment: (1) to prevent a repetition; (2) to deter others—the threat of

---

23. Stanley Benn, "Punishment," in *The Encyclopedia of Philosophy*, ed. Paul Edwards (Macmillan, 1967), 29–35.

punishment deters potential offenders; and (3) to rehabilitate the criminal (this need not be seen as punishment, but it may involve that).

The threat of punishment is everything. Every act of punishment is to that extent an admission of the failure of the threat. If the threat were successful, no punishment would be needed, and the question of justification would not arise.

One problem with the utilitarian theory is simply that it goes against our notion of desert. It says that social utility is a necessary condition for punishment. But I would be in favor of punishing at least the most egregious offenders even if I knew they would never commit another crime. Suppose we discovered Adolf Hitler living quietly in a small Argentine town and were sure that no good (in terms of deterrence or prevention) would come of punishing him. Shouldn't we still bring him to trial and punish him appropriately?

A further problem is that utilitarianism would seem to enjoin punishment for prospective crimes. If the best evidence we have leads us to believe that some person or group of people will commit a crime, we are justified in applying punitive measures if our actions satisfy a cost-benefit analysis.

The main weakness of utilitarianism is that it seems to allow the punishment of the innocent if that will deter others from crime. We want only criminals punished, but utilitarians focus on results, not justice. If we can frame an innocent bum for a rape and murder in order to prevent a riot, the utilitarian will be tempted to do so. This violates the essence of justice.

Some philosophers, namely Anthony Quinton, Stanley Benn, and R. S. Peters, have rejected this criticism as missing the point of what punishment is. They contend that punishment is logically connected with committing a crime, so that the one punished must be presumed guilty.[24] But this "definitional stop" only moves the problem to a different dimension with-

---

24. Anthony Quinton, "Punishment," in *Philosophy, Politics and Society*, ed. P. Laslett, 1959; Stanley Benn and R. S. Peters admit that "If utilitarianism could really be shown to involve punishing the innocent, or a false parade of punishment, or punishment in anticipation of an offense, these criticisms would no doubt be conclusive. They are, however, based on a misconception of what the utilitarian theory is about. We said at the beginning of this chapter that 'punishment' implied in its primary sense, not the inflicting of *any* sort of suffering, but inflicting suffering under certain specified conditions, one of which was that it must be for a breach of a rule" ("The Utilitarian Case for Deterrence," 98).

out solving it. Suppose we call "punishment" punishing the guilty and give another name, such as "telishment" (Rawls's suggestion), to judicially harming the innocent for deterrent purposes. Now the question becomes "Should we ever telish people?" The utilitarian is committed to telishment—whenever the aggregate utility warrants it.

While these criticisms are severe, they do not overthrow utilitarianism altogether. One surely admits that penal law should have a deterrent effect. The point seems to be that utilitarian theories need a retributive base on which to build. I will comment on this point later.

Rehabilitative Theories

According to rehabilitative theories, crime is a disease, and the criminal is a sick person who needs to be cured, not punished. Such rehabilitationists as B. F. Skinner, Karl Menninger, and Benjamin Karpman point to the failure and cruelties of our penal system and advocate an alternative of therapy and reconditioning. "Therapy not torture" might be said to be their motto for criminals are not really in control of their behavior but are suffering personality disorders. Crime is, by and large, a result of an adverse early environment, so that what must be done is to recondition the criminal through positive reinforcement. Punishment is a prescientific response to antisocial behavior. At best punishment temporarily suppresses adverse behavior, but, if untreated, Skinner argues, it will resurface again as though the punishment never occurred. It is useless as a deterrent. Rehabilitationists charge that retributivists are guilty of holding an antiquated notion of human beings as possessing free wills and being responsible for their behavior. We, including all of our behavior, are all products of our heredity and, especially, our environment.

> Menninger sees rehabilitation as a replacement for the concept of justice in criminal procedure: The very word *justice* irritates scientists. No surgeon expects to be asked if an operation for cancer is just or not. No doctor will be reproached on the grounds that the dose of penicillin he has prescribed is less or more than *justice* would stipulate. . . . It does not advance a solution to use the word *justice*. It is a subjective emotional word. . . . The concept is so vague, so distorted in its application, so hypocritical, and usually so irrelevant that it offers no help in the solution of the crime problem which it exists to combat but results in its exact opposite—injustice, injustice to everybody.[25]

---

25. Karl Menninger, *The Crime of Punishment* (Viking Press, 1968), 17, 10–11. The passage is remarkable for its apparent denial and assertion of the objective reality of justice.

Of course we need to confine criminals for their own good and society's, but a process of positive reinforcement must be the means of dealing with criminals and their "crimes." Karpman, one of the proponents of this theory, puts it this way:

> Basically, criminality is but a symptom of insanity, using the term in its widest generic sense to express unacceptable social behavior based on unconscious motivation flowing from a disturbed instinctive and emotional life, whether this appears in frank psychoses, or in less obvious form in neuroses and unrecognized psychoses. . . . If criminals are products of early environmental influences in the same sense that psychotics and neurotics are, then it should be possible to reach them psychotherapeutically.[26]

Let me begin my criticism of rehabilitation by relating a retelling of the Good Samaritan story. You recall that a Jew went down from Jerusalem to Jericho and fell among thieves who beat him, robbed him, and left him dying. A priest and a Levite passed by him but an outcast Samaritan came to his rescue, bringing him to a hotel for treatment and paying his bills.

A contemporary version of the story goes like this. A man is brutally robbed and left on the side of the road by his assailants. A priest comes by but regrets having to leave the man in his condition, in order to avoid being late for the church service he must lead. Likewise, a lawyer passes by, rushing to meet a client. Finally, a psychiatrist sees our subject, rushes over to him, places the man's head in his lap and in a distraught voice cries out, "Oh, this is awful! How deplorable! Tell me, sir, who did this to you? He needs help."

Not all psychiatrists fit this description of mislocating the victim, but the story cannot be dismissed as merely a joke in poor taste. It fits an attitude that substitutes the concept of sickness for moral failure. Let me briefly note some of the problems with the whole theory of rehabilitation as a substitute for punishment. First, this doctrine undermines the very notion of human autonomy and responsibility. Individuals who are not mentally ill are free agents whose actions should be taken seriously as flowing from free decisions.[27] If a person kills in cold blood, he or she

---

26. Benjamin Karpman, "Criminal Psychodynamics," *Journal of Criminal Law and Criminology* 47 (1956): 9. See also B. F. Skinner, *Science and Human Behavior* (Macmillan, 1953), 182–193.

27. I am assuming that the case for free will and responsibility is cogent. For a good discussion see the readings by Harry Frankfurt, Gary Watson, and Peter van

must bear the responsibility for that murder. Rehabilitation theories reduce moral problems to medical problems.

Furthermore, rehabilitation doesn't seem to work. Rehabilitation is a form of socialization through sophisticated medical treatment. While humans are malleable, there are limits to what socialization and medical technology can do. Socialization can be relatively effective in infancy and early childhood, less so in late childhood, while even less effective in adulthood. Perhaps at some future time when brain manipulation becomes possible, we will make greater strides toward behavior modification. Perhaps we will be able to plant electrodes in a criminal's brain and so affect his cerebral cortex that he "repents" of his crime and is restored to society. The question then will be whether we have a right to tamper with someone's psyche in this manner. Furthermore, would a neurologically induced repentance for a crime really be repentance—or would it be an overriding of the criminal's autonomy and personality? And won't that tampering itself be a form of punishment?

Conclusion

Let me bring this part of our work to a close by suggesting that there are elements of truth in all three theories of punishment. Rehabilitationism, insofar as it seeks to restore the criminal to society as a morally whole being, has merit as an aspect of the penal process, but it cannot stand alone. Retributivism is surely correct to make guilt a necessary condition for punishment and to seek to make the punishment fit the crime. Its emphasis on desert is vital to our theory of reward and punishment, and with this it respects humans as rational, responsible agents, who should be treated in a manner fitting to their deserts. But it may be too rigid in its *retrospective* gaze and in need of mercy and *prospective* vision. Utilitarianism seems correct in emphasizing this prospective feature of treatment with the goal of promoting human flourishing. But it is in danger of manipulating people for the social good—even of punishing the innocent or punishing the guilty more than they deserve (for social purposes). One way of combining retributivism and utilitarianism has been suggested by John Rawls in his classic essay, "Two Concepts of Rules." Rawls attempts

Inwagen in *Moral Responsibility*, ed. John Martin Fischer (Ithaca: Cornell University Press, 1986).

to do justice to both the retributive and the utilitarian theories of punishment.[28] He argues that there is a difference between justifying an institution and justifying a given instance where the institution is applied. The question "Why do we have law or system?" is of a different nature from the question "Why are we applying the law in the present situation in this mode?" Applied to punishment: (1) "Why do we have a system of punishment?" and (2) "Why are we harming John for his misdeed?" are two different sorts of questions. When we justify the institution of punishment, we resort to utilitarian or consequentialist considerations: A society in which the wicked prosper will offer inadequate inducement to virtue. A society in which some rules are made and enforced will get on better than a society in which no rules exist or are enforced. But when we seek to justify an individual application of punishment, we resort to retributivist considerations; for example, when someone commits a breach against the law, that person merits a fitting punishment.

So we can operate on two levels. On the second-order (reflective) level we accept rule utilitarianism and acknowledge that the penal law should serve society's overall good. In order to do this we need a retributive system—one that adheres to common ideas of fair play and desert. So rule utilitarianism on the second-order level yields retributivism on the first-order level. As we have noted, some have interpreted this process to entail that there is no noninstitutional or natural desert or justice, but that these things only come into being by social choice. It is more accurate to say that there is a primordial or deontological idea of desert which needs social choice to become activated or institutionalized for human purposes. It is not as though society could rationally choose some other practice, but that, if it is to choose rationally—to promote its goals of flourishing and resolving conflicts of interest—it must choose to reward and punish according to one's desert.

Part II: Capital Punishment

The small crowd that gathered outside the prison to protest the execution of Steven Judy softly sang, "We Shall Overcome" . . . But it didn't seem quite the same hearing it sung out of concern for someone who, on finding a woman with a flat tire, raped and murdered

---

28. John Rawls, "Two Concepts of Justice," *Philosophical Review* (1955).

her and drowned her three small children, then said that he hadn't been "losing any sleep" over his crimes. . . .

I remember the grocer's wife. She was a plump, happy woman who enjoyed the long workday she shared with her husband in their ma-and-pa store. One evening, two young men came in and showed guns, and the grocer gave them everything in the cash register.

For no reason, almost as an afterthought, one of the men shot the grocer in the face. The woman stood only a few feet from her husband when he was turned into a dead, bloody mess.

She was about 50 when it happened. In a few years her mind was almost gone, and she looked 80. They might as well have killed her too.

Then there was the woman I got to know after her daughter was killed by a wolfpack gang during a motoring trip. The mother called me occasionally, but nothing that I said could ease her torment. It ended when she took her own life.

A couple of years ago I spent a long evening with the husband, sister and parents of a fine young woman who had been forced into the trunk of a car in a hospital parking lot. The degenerate who kidnapped her kept her in the trunk, like an ant in a jar, until he got tired of the game. Then he killed her."[29]

Who so sheddeth man's blood, by man shall his blood be shed. (Genesis 9:6)

Proponents of capital punishment justify it from either a retributive or a utilitarian framework, sometimes using both theories for a combined justification. Abolitionists deny that these arguments for capital punishment are sound, because the sanctity of human life which gives each person a right to life is inconsistent with the practice of putting criminals to death.

As we noted in Part I, the retributivist argues (1) that all the guilty deserve to be punished; (2) that only the guilty deserve to be punished; and (3) that the guilty deserve a punishment proportional in severity to their crime. It follows that all those who commit capital offenses deserve capital punishments. This is the idea suggested in the quotation from the Bible at the beginning of this part of our work, assuming that malice aforethought is present.

---

29. Mike Royko, quoted in Michael Moore, "The Moral Worth of Retributivism" in *Punishment and Rehabilitation,* ed. Jeffrie G. Murphy, 3d. ed. (Wadsworth, 1995): 98–99.

A classic expression of the retributivist position on capital punishment is Kant's statement that if an offender, "has committed murder, he must *die.* In this case, no possible substitute can satisfy justice. For there is no *parallel* between death and even the most miserable life, so that there is no equality of crime and retribution unless the perpetrator is judicially put to death (at all events without any maltreatment which might make humanity an object of horror in the person of the sufferer)."

As quoted in Part I, Kant illustrates the doctrine of exact retribution:

> Even if a civil society were to dissolve itself with the consent of all its members (for example, if a people who inhabited an island decided to separate and disperse to other parts of the world), the last murderer in prison would first have to be executed in order that each should receive his just deserts and that the people should not bear the guilt of a capital crime through failing to insist on its punishment; for if they do not do so, they can be regarded as accomplices in the public violation of justice.[30]

For Kant the death penalty was a conclusion of the argument for justice: just recompense to the victim and just punishment to the offender. As a person of dignity, the victim deserves (as a kind of compensatory justice) to have the offender harmed in proportion to the gravity of the crime, and as a person of high worth and responsibility, the offender shows himself or herself deserving of capital punishment.

Let us expand on the retributivist argument. Each person has a right to life. But criminal C violates an innocent person V's right to life by threatening it or by killing V. The threat to V constitutes a grave offense, but taking V's life constitutes a capital offense. Attempting to take V's life, from a moral point of view, is equivalent to taking his or her life. Therefore C deserves to be put to death for the offense.

But the abolitionist responds, "No, putting the criminal to death only compounds evil. If killing is an evil, then the state actually doubles the evil by executing the murderer. The state violates the criminal's right to life. It carries out *legalized murder.*" To quote the famous eighteenth-century abolitionist Cesare di Beccaria, "The death penalty cannot be useful because of the example of barbarity it gives to men . . . it seems to me absurd that the laws . . . which punish homicide should themselves commit it."[31]

---

30. Immanuel Kant, *The Metaphysics of Morals,* trans. John Ladd (Indianapolis: Bobbs-Merrill, 1965), 103.

31. Cesare di Beccaria, *Of Crimes and Punishments,* trans. Henry Paolucci (Indianapolis: Bobbs-Merrill, 1963, originally published 1764).

But the abolitionist is mistaken on two counts. First, the state does not violate the criminal's right to life, for the right to life (more precisely, the right not to be killed) is not an absolute right which can never be overridden (or forfeited).[32] If the right to life were absolute, we could not kill aggressors even when it was necessary to defend our lives or those of our loved ones. It is a *prima facie* or conditional right which can be overridden by a more weighty moral reason. Our right to life, liberty and property is connected with our duty to respect the rights of others to life, liberty and property. By violating the right of another to liberty, I thereby forfeit my right to liberty. By violating the right of another to property, I thereby forfeit my property right. Similarly, by violating the right of another to life, I thereby forfeit my right to life. Violating the victim's right to life is a sufficient reason for overriding the criminal's prima facie right to life. The criminal in murdering the innocent victim has made himself vulnerable to the state's authority to use the sword in behalf of justice and self-defense.

On the retributivist account, this forfeiture of the criminal's right to life only tells part of the story. Forfeiture gives the moral and legal authority the right to inflict the criminal with a punishment, but it says nothing about the *duty* of the authority to punish. The principle of just desert completes the theory of retribution. Not only do murderers forfeit their right to life, but they positively deserve their punishment. If they have committed a capital offense, they deserve a capital punishment. If first-degree murder is on the level of the worst types of crimes, as we think it is, then we are justified in imposing the worst type of punishments on the murderer. Death would be the fitting punishment; anything less would

---

32. In this essay I speak of the *forfeiting* or the *overriding* of a right to life as interchangeable, though they are not the same thing. I may forfeit my right to drive by violating laws against drinking alcohol while driving, but my right to drive the family car today may be overridden by my father's need to take it to work. If one thinks of a right not to be killed as natural right which society cannot override, as Kant seems to, the only way it can be morally undermined is by one's own immoral acts. The criminal forfeits his right to freedom or life. A consequentialist or contractualist may argue that the right not to be killed is only a prima facie right that can be overridden for good moral reasons, one of which is the murdering of another person. Since I think that all three theories justify the death penalty for murder, I am not taking sides between them in this work—except to insist that even in utilitarian defenses a retributive core must be present in terms of the criminal doing something to deserve what he or she gets.

indicate that we regarded murder a less serious offense. So the abolitionist is mistaken in holding that killing is always wrong. Killing may be an evil, but, if so, it is a lesser evil when carried out as an act of retributivist justice. A greater evil would be to permit the guilty to go unpunished or improperly punished.

We do know of crimes worse than murder—repeatedly torturing victims over a long period of time and driving them insane is worse than murdering them. A thoroughgoing retributivist might well advocate legal punishment consisting of torturing torturers and rapists (probably using machines so as to distance the retributivist as far as possible from the repulsive nature of the punishment). The ancient biblical *lex talionis*, discussed in Part I, demands an equivalent punishment to that of the crime itself. In the context of purposefully harming others, the passage reads: "Thou shalt give life for life, an eye for an eye, a tooth for a tooth, a hand for a hand, burning for burning, wound for wound, stripe for stripe" (Exod. 21:23–25). Accordingly, the torturer should be tortured exactly to the severity that he tortured the victim, the rapist should be raped, and the cheater should have an equivalent harm inflicted upon him or her. The criminals deserve such punishment, as it reflects the principle of proportionality.

As we argued in Part I, the principle of desert can be overridden by other considerations, and good reasons exist for not always giving the criminal all he or she deserves. How could we punish Hitler, Eichmann, Stalin, or a serial killer in proportion to the gravity of their offenses? There are limits to what punishment can and should do. In some cases, e.g., serial murder, giving the criminal precisely what he deserves is impossible; and since we are under no obligation to do the impossible (*ultra posse nemo obligatur*), we do not always have an obligation to give people what they deserve.[33] Although Hitler and the serial killer surely deserve more than the death penalty, it's hard to say how much more. Our intuitions are unclear on how to determine anything more than the death penalty, so we tend to accept that as the upper limit—even though both retributivism and deterrence might be served by these harsher punishments.

Part of our reluctance to be consistent retributivists may be cultural,

---

33. There is an asymmetry between reward and punishment. A beneficiary of a reward has the right to decline the reward, but the recipient of a deserved punishment has no such option. On the other hand, a more stringent obligation exists to give people what they positively deserve than what they negatively deserve. We can forgive those who trespass against us.

rather than strictly (or objectively) moral. Killing and torturing are vile acts, and we—most educated people in Western society at least—shudder at the thought of doing these things to others, even though we agree they deserve them. As war veterans know, killing, even in a just war, exacts a psychological toll. It may have a "brutalization" effect. Let us call these psychological factors *external considerations* against exacting equivalence of punishment to crime. At any rate, because of a slow trend towards non-violence in much of our society, corporal punishment, torture, and executions have become increasing unpopular. Whippings, burnings, and torture have been declared too vile a response to the criminal. The death penalty is the sole remaining corporal penalty, and we have striven to make it as painless as possible (another paradox for retributivists and deterrentists). The question is whether something less than death would do as well, say, long-term prison sentences. A mild retributivist might allow mercy to enter the picture earlier, perhaps advocating long prison sentences. But for most retributivists, like myself, death seems an appropriate punishment for the worst types of crimes—though, strictly speaking, it may not be anywhere near to the proportion of suffering or evil done by the criminal.[34] Anything more (e.g., torture), though perhaps deserved in some cases, would have unacceptable social costs. Anything less would be a failure to approximate justice and carry out minimally adequate deterrence.

If a society is secure, it might well opt to show mercy and not execute murderers. At this point utilitarian reasons may mitigate retributive judgments, inclining the state towards lesser punishments, not because the criminal doesn't deserve the death penalty, but because a secure society isn't threatened as a whole by occasional murders, heinous though they be. In a secure society (Scandinavian countries, Switzerland, the Netherlands, and Austria come to mind—with crime rates a tiny fraction of that of the United States) capital offenses are not tearing away at the very fabric of the social order.[35] However, given the justice of death as a fitting moral

---

34. Most debates center on whether the death penalty is appropriate for first-degree murder. It is confined to murder and espionage in federal and most state laws. I would consider it for white-collar crimes where powerful government officials or business people abuse their power, betray the public trust, and do irrevocable harm to those beholden to them. For example, bank presidents or executives who embezzle from those who have entrusted to them their savings both deserve and might be deterred by the threat of the death penalty.

35. Perhaps we ought to err on the side of mercy and reform, but there seem

response to capital crimes, the burden of proof for overriding the death penalty in capital offense cases rests with the abolitionist. If the forfeiture of right argument and the desert argument, sketched above, are sound, the murderer has forfeited his right to life and the death penalty is deserved. As such the death penalty is not only a morally permissible act, but a prima facie duty, which may be overridden only for good reasons.

Retributivism and the Rehabilitative Penance Model of Punishment

Recently, several philosophers, including Herbert Morris, Margaret Falls, and Anthony Duff, have put forth a version of retributivism that, as retributive, emphasizes desert, but also appeals to the idea of inherent human dignity to put severe limits on punishment, prohibiting capital punishment. The goal of punishment is penance, not death.

Duff holds that punishment must be a form of communication to the criminal, expressing moral condemnation for the deed and calling the culprit to repent. The criminal's autonomy and dignity must be preserved in the punitive process. A necessary condition for this preservation of dignity and autonomy is that the criminal recognize what he or she has done, acknowledge his or her guilt, and repent of the crime. It follows that we may not put the murderer to death, for that precludes the opportunity for repentance and restoration to the community. The penance model is a sophisticated version of the rehabilitation theory of punishment, discussed in Part I. It is more cogent than the usual rehabilitative theories in that it links retribution with rehabilitation.

One corollary of this view, set forth by Duff, states that if the criminal becomes insane or amnesiac after the crime, he cannot be punished.[36] I find this counterintuitive and a clue as to why this theory is mistaken. Suppose we developed a pill (or a way of using electrodes on parts of

---

to be times when this is not feasible—either because the criminal is beyond the pale of reform or because of the social costs.

"There but for the grace of God go I." I feel this sentiment too. There is some luck in not being evil—for which we should be eternally grateful, and this may mitigate our rage at evildoers, but it should not cancel it altogether. If I did a dastardly act, I would expect you to sympathize ("There but for the grace of God go I") but still execute me. I'm still deserving of the death penalty.

36. Anthony Duff, "Expression, Penance and Reform," in Jeffrie Murphy, ed. *Punishment and Rehabilitation,* 3d. ed. (Wadsworth, 1995), 169–198.

the brain) that would cause selective amnesia. Criminal Charley has just committed cold-blooded murder. Now he takes the pill which will elimi-nate the memory of his deed (as well as his putting the pill in his mouth). The result: success. Charley no longer remembers what he did. But would he not still deserve severe punishment?

There is no incompatibility between penance and desert. I may repent of my sins and immoral deeds and still acknowledge that I deserve to be punished for them. In fact, the very nature of repenting includes a sense of deserving to suffer for wrongdoing. The convicted murderer Gary Gil-more requested that he be executed for his heinous murders, holding that he deserved nothing less than death.

Perhaps religious people will insist that criminals, no matter how low they sink, still possess the image of God. In this spirit, the Christian philos-opher Margaret Falls argues movingly that treating people as moral agents prohibits us from executing them. "Holding an offender responsible nec-essarily includes demanding that she respond as only moral agents can: by reevaluating her behavior. If the punishment meted out makes reflective response to it impossible, then it is not a demand for response as a moral agent. Death is not a punishment to which reflective moral response is possible. . . . Death terminates the possibility of moral reform."[37]

To Falls's argument that the death penalty makes moral reform impossi-ble, two things must be said: (1) It's false, and (2) it's not an argument for the complete abolition of capital punishment.

(1) Regarding the claim that it's false, the criminal may be given time to repent of his or her offense before execution. It is hard to know when the murderer has truly repented and has been rehabilitated, since faking it is in the murderer's self-interest, but even if he does repent, the heinous-ness of the deed remains and he should receive his just desert. Indeed, given my Golden Rule argument (discussed below), one would expect the repentant murderer to agree that he or she deserved to die and, as Gary Gilmore did, request execution. (2) Regarding my second claim, even if some offenders were suitably rehabilitated, and even if we had a policy of showing mercy to those who gave strong evidence of having been morally reformed, many criminals may well be incurable, given our present means for rehabilitation and moral reform. Present rehabilitation programs are

---

37. Margaret Falls, "Against the Death Penalty: A Christian Stance in a Secular World," *Christian Century* (December 10, 1986), 1118, 1119.

not very successful. In fact, I doubt whether it is the primary goal of the criminal justice system to engage in rehabilitation. Its primary goal is to protect society and carry out justice, though if it can aid in reforming the prisoner, so much the better. The point is, failure to reform the criminal need not be proof that the system is unjust.

Here is a paradox for the abolitionist: *Either* the murderer is a free being with inherent dignity and so may be held accountable for his crime to the point of being executed for it, *or* the murderer is not a free being with inherent dignity and so does not deserve any special protection as possessing positive value. He may be killed as would be a rabid dog, man-eating tiger, or a dangerous virus. Either way, the death penalty seems fair. Let me elaborate on this paradox.

Elsewhere, I have argued that, although a popular dogma, the secular doctrine that all humans have equal *positive* worth is groundless. The notion of equal worth, perhaps the most misused term in our moral vocabulary, is a derivation from a past religious age (assuming that our age is secular) when people believed that human beings were endowed with a soul possessing the infinite image of God. The statement in the Declaration of Independence that "all men are created equal" entails a Creator, which plays no role in the secularist's theory of justice. We may, of course, be equally worthless, but I know of no account that gives us both a notion of positive worth and an equal distribution of that quality. Some philosophers say that our ability to reason gives us inherent worth, but if it does, then surely we are radically unequal, as anyone who has graded philosophy papers or observed people reasoning knows. We may apply the *principle of impartiality* and judge people by equal laws and by the same moral code, but then the resulting evaluations of people will be vastly different. As in grading students' tests and course work, some will get high marks in the moral-evaluation and some will fail. Generally, we can say that a person's worth is grounded in such things as his or her moral character and contribution to society (it may include the global society, including nonhuman animals).[38]

If our moral status is largely what gives us worth, it would follow that people like Jeffrey Dahmer, Ted Bundy, Steven Judy, Adolf Hitler, Hein-

---

38. See my "A Critique of Contemporary Egalitarianism," *Faith and Philosophy* 8, no. 4 (1991), and my "Theories of Equality: A Critical Analysis," *Behavior and Philosophy* 23, no. 2 (Summer 1995).

rich Himmler, and Joseph Stalin, who are grossly immoral, who sadistically harm others, who with malice aforethought commit or order others to commit violent crimes, are evil. They have *negative* worth. Many criminals, even if they are leaders of nations, may be morally incurable. A tradition, going back at least to Plato, states that even as the life of a person with an incurably diseased body is not worth living, so the life of a person with an incurably diseased soul is not worth living. Speaking of the pilot of a ferry who conveys people across a river to their destination, Plato says:

> [The pilot] knows that if anyone afflicted in the body with serious and incurable disease has escaped drowning, the man is wretched for not having died and has received no benefit from him [the pilot]. He therefore reckons that if any man suffers many incurable diseases in the soul, which is so much more precious than the body, for such a man life is not worth living and it will be no benefit to him if he, the pilot, saves him from the sea or from the law court or from any other risk. For he knows it is not better for an evil man to live, for he must needs live ill.[39]

In the *Laws* Plato says that the execution of an incurable criminal is a double blessing to the community: "It will be a lesson to them to keep themselves from wrong, and it will rid society of an evil man. These are reasons for which a legislator is bound to ordain the chastisement of death for such desperate villainies and for them alone."[40]

I am not arguing for this position, only suggesting that it is a cogent implication not only of a Platonic thesis that some people have evil souls, but also of a secular view of humanity as an animal who has evolved by accident from "lower" animals over time. If humans do not possess some kind of intrinsic value—say the image of God—then why not rid ourselves of those who egregiously violate the necessary conditions for civilized living, our moral and legal codes? How are sadistic murderers of more worth than a rabid dog, a man-eating tiger or the HIV virus?

So my challenge to the abolitionist stands. If the religious view is correct, and we have a dignity that is based on a transcendent trait, then the fact that we have freely killed a child of God leads to the judgment that we deserve to be executed for our malicious act. But if secularism is correct and we have no value apart from our moral character and social function,

---

39. Plato, *Gorgias* 512a (see also *Gorgias* 425c).
40. Plato, *Laws* 862d.

then many criminals manifest a corrupt soul and are the embodiment of evil, so destroying them is good riddance to bad rubbish. It is prudent to destroy what is evil. Besides, it isn't as though we are doing to the criminal anything that will not happen in a few years anyway. In the end we all rot—unless there is something more to life than the secularist supposes.

Either way, it seems we may justifiably execute the murderer.[41] Yet there is another reason why we should favor the death penalty: the value of deterrence.

Deterrence

The utilitarian argument for capital punishment is that it deters would-be offenders from committing first degree murder. Thorstein Sellin's study of comparing states with and without capital punishment concludes that the death penalty is not a better deterrent of homicides than imprisonment.[42] On the other hand, Isaac Ehrlich's study, the most thorough study to date, takes into account the problems of complex sociological data in terms of race, heredity, regional lines, standards of housing, education, opportunities, cultural patterns, intelligence, and so forth, and concludes that the death penalty does deter. His simultaneous equation regression model suggests that over the period 1933–1969 "an additional execution per year . . . may have resulted on the average in 7 or 8 fewer murders."[43] It should be noted that Ehrlich began his study as an abolitionist, but his data forced him to change his position. However, Ehrlich's study has been criticized, largely for technical reasons, so that his conclusion that we have significant statistical evidence that the death penalty deters better than

---

41. The paradox should be qualified. If the criminal has the same status as a rabid dog, we do not have an obligation to kill him. We can isolate him somewhere. But, the question arises, if he, indeed, has no moral status, why waste any resources on him at all? He has no right not to be killed. Some, including Tziporah Kasachkoff and John Kleinig have urged that we ought to adhere to the principle "use no more force than is necessary to get the job done." But I see no reason to adhere to this principle in this sort of case. It may be that with regard to rabid dogs the principle doesn't obtain. Or in cases of criminals, it may be that more, rather than less, force is deserved.

42. Thorstein Sellin, *The Death Penalty* (1959) reprinted in *The Death Penalty in America*, ed. Hugo Bedau (Anchor Books, 1967).

43. Isaac Ehrlich, "The Deterrent Effect of Capital Punishment: A Question of Life and Death," *American Economic Review* 65 (June 1975): 397–417.

prison sentences is not conclusive.[44] The problems seem to be that there are simply too many variables to control in comparing demographic patterns (culture, heredity, poverty, education, religion, and general environmental factors) and that the death penalty isn't carried out frequently enough to have the effect that it might have under circumstances of greater use. One criticism of Ehrlich's work is that if he had omitted the years 1962 to 1969, he would have had significantly different results. David Baldus and James Cole contend that Ehrlich omitted salient variables, such as the rate of migration from rural to urban areas. On the other hand, Stephen Layson's study in 1985 corroborates Ehrlich's conclusion, except that Layson's work indicates that each time the death penalty is applied, the murder rate is reduced by about eighteen murders.[45] A consensus is wanting, so that at present we must conclude that we lack strong statistical evidence that capital punishment deters. But this should not be construed as evidence against the deterrence thesis. There is no such evidence for nondeterrence either. The statistics available are simply inconclusive either way.

Precisely on the basis of this inconclusivity with regard to the evidence, some abolitionists, for example, Stephen Nathanson, argue that deterrence cannot be the moral basis for capital punishment. "The death penalty can be justified as analogous to defensive killing only if it can be shown that it does save lives. Since that has not been shown, one cannot appeal to this protective function as providing a moral basis for executing murderers."[46] I think Nathanson is wrong about this. There is some nonstatistical evidence based on common sense that gives credence to the hypothe-

---

44. See for example David Baldus and James Cole, "A Comparison of the Work of Thorstein Sellin and Isaac Ehrlich on the Deterrent Effect of Capital Punishment," *Yale Law Journal* 85 (1975).

45. Stephen Layson, "Homicide and Deterrence: A Reexamination of the United States Time-Series Evidence," *Southern Economic Journal* (1985): 68, 80.

46. Stephen Nathanson, *An Eye for an Eye?* (Lanham, Md.: Rowman & Littlefield, 1987). See chap. 2 for the abolitionist's argument. Actually Nathanson admits the deterrent effect of the death penalty. On p. 17 he says "I doubt that anyone would deny that the death penalty deters some murderers, if this means only that fewer murders would occur in a situation where the death penalty was imposed than in a situation in which murderers suffered no punishment at all." The question seems to be whether long term imprisonment doesn't do as well. Although I shall take issue with many of the arguments in Nathanson's book, I regard it as one of the best defenses of abolitionism.

sis that the threat of the death penalty deters and that it does so better than long prison sentences. I will discuss the commonsense case below, but first I want to present an argument for the deterrent effect of capital punishment that is agnostic as to whether the death penalty deters better than lesser punishments.[47]

Ernest van den Haag has set forth what he calls the Best Bet Argument.[48] He argues that even though we don't know for certain whether the death penalty deters or prevents other murders, we should bet that it does. Indeed, due to our ignorance, any social policy we take is a gamble. Not to choose capital punishment for first-degree murder is as much a bet that capital punishment doesn't deter as choosing the policy is a bet that it does. There is a significant difference in the betting, however, in that to bet against capital punishment is to bet against the innocent and for the murderer, while to bet for it is to bet against the murderer and for the innocent.[49]

The point is this: We are accountable for what we let happen, as well as for what we actually do. If I fail to bring up my children properly, so that they are a menace to society, I am to some extent responsible for their bad

---

47. Ibid., 31.

48. Ernest van den Haag, "On Deterrence and the Death Penalty," *Ethics* 78 (July 1968).

49. The Best Bet argument rejects the passive/active distinction involved in killing and letting die. Many people think that it is far worse to kill someone than to let him die—even with the same motivation. More generally, they hold that it is worse to *do* something bad than *allowing* something bad to happen. I think people feel this way because they are tacitly supposing different motivational stances. Judith Jarvis Thomson gives the following counterexample to this doctrine. John is a trolley driver who suddenly realizes that his brakes have failed. He is heading for a group of workers on the track before him and will certainly kill them if something isn't done immediately. Fortunately, there is a side track to the right onto which John can turn the trolley. Unfortunately, there is one worker on that track who will be killed if John steers the trolley onto the side track.Now if the passive/active distinction holds, John should do nothing but simply allow the trolley to take its toll of the five men on the track before him. But that seems terrible. Surely, by turning quickly and causing the trolley to move onto the side track John will be saving a total of four lives. It seems morally preferable for John to turn the trolley onto the side track and actively cause the death of one man rather than passively allow the death of five. John is caught in a situation in which he cannot help doing or allowing harm, but he can act so that the lesser of the evils obtains—rather than the greater of the evils.

behavior. I could have caused it to be somewhat better. If I have good evidence that a bomb will blow up the building you are working in and fail to notify you (assuming I can), I am partly responsible for your death, if and when the bomb explodes. So we are responsible for what we omit doing, as well as for what we do. Purposefully to refrain from a lesser evil which we know will allow a greater evil to occur is to be at least partially responsible for the greater evil. This responsibility for our omissions underlies van den Haag's argument, to which we now return.

Suppose that we choose a policy of capital punishment for capital crimes. In this case we are betting that the death of some murderers will be more than compensated for by the lives of some innocents not being murdered (either by these murderers or others who would have murdered). If we're right, we have saved the lives of the innocent. If we're wrong, unfortunately, we've sacrificed the lives of some murderers. But say we choose not to have a social policy of capital punishment. If capital punishment doesn't work as a deterrent, we've come out ahead, but if it does work, then we've missed an opportunity to save innocent lives. If we value the saving of innocent lives more highly than the loss of the guilty, then to bet on a policy of capital punishment turns out to be rational. The reasoning goes like this. Let "CP" stand for "capital punishment":

THE WAGER

	CP works	*CP doesn't work*
We bet on CP	a. We win: Some murderers die & innocents are saved.	b. We lose: Some murderers die for no purpose.
We bet against CP	c. We lose: Murderers live & innocents needlessly die.	d. We win: Murderers live & some lives of others are unaffected.

Suppose that we estimate that the utility value of a murderer's life is 5, while the value of an innocent's life is 10. (Although we cannot give lives exact numerical values, we can make rough comparative estimates of value—e.g. Mother Teresa's life is more valuable than Adolf Hitler's; all things being equal, the life of an innocent person has at least twice the value of a murderer's life. My own sense is that the murderer has forfeited most, if not all, of his worth, but if I had to put a ratio to it, it would be 1,000 to 1.) Given van den Haag's figures, the sums work out this way:

A murderer saved	+5
A murderer executed	−5
An innocent saved	+10
An innocent murdered	−10

Suppose that for each execution only two innocent lives are spared. Then the outcomes (correlating to the above wager table) read as follows:

a. $-5 + 20 = +15$

b. -5

c. $+5 - 20 = -15$

d. $+5$

If all the possibilities are roughly equal, we can sum their outcomes like this:

If we bet on capital punishment, (a) and (b) obtain $= +10$

If we bet against capital punishment (c) and (d) obtain $= -10$.

So to execute convicted murderers turns out to be a good bet. To abolish the death penalty for convicted murderers would be a bad bet. We unnecessarily put the innocent at risk.

Even if we value the utility of an innocent life only slightly more than that of a murderer, it is still rational to execute convicted murderers. As van den Haag writes, "Though we have no proof of the positive deterrence of the penalty, we also have no proof of zero or negative effectiveness. I believe we have no right to risk additional future victims of murder for the sake of sparing convicted murderers; on the contrary, our moral obligation is to risk the possible ineffectiveness of executions."[50]

A Critique of the Best Bet Argument

The abolitionist David Conway has constructed an instructive, imaginary dialogue about van den Haag's argument in which an opponent (O) objects to this line of reasoning, contending that the gambling metaphor regarding capital punishment (C.P.) is misleading, for it seems to devalue the lives of the guilty. We ought not to gamble with human lives. The issue is between the *possibility* of saving some lives (if deterrence works) and the *certainty* of sacrificing some lives (whether or not it works). Con-

---

50. Ernest van den Haag, "On Deterrence."

way's proponent (P) for van den Haag's argument counters that gambling can be interpreted as doing a cost-benefit analysis with regard to saving lives. Here is a segment of Conway's dialogue:

> P: [T]here are other circumstances in which we must gamble with lives in this way. Suppose you were almost, but not quite certain that a madman was about to set off all the bombs in the Western hemisphere. On [your] principle [that we ought not gamble with human life], you would not be justified in shooting him, even if it were the only possible way to stop him.
> O: Yes, I suppose that I must grant you that. But perhaps my suppositions that gambling is taking the risk and that gambling with human lives is wrong, taken together, at least partially account for my intuitive revulsion with van den Haag's argument.
> P: That may be. But so far, your intuitions have come to nothing in producing a genuine objection to the argument. I might add that I cannot even agree with your intuition that not gambling is taking the sure thing. Don't we sometimes disapprove of the person who refuses to take out life insurance or automobile insurance on the grounds that he is unwisely gambling that he will not die prematurely or be responsible for a highway accident? And he is taking the sure thing, keeping the premium money in his pocket. So, in common sense terms, failure to take a wise bet is sometimes "gambling."
> O: You are right again. . . . But that does not change my views about C.P. Once the bet is clarified, it should be clear that you are asking us to risk too much, to actually take a human life on far too small a chance of saving others. It is just a rotten bet.
> P: But it is not. As I have said, the life of each murderer is clearly worth much less than the life of an innocent, and, besides, each criminal life lost may save many innocents.

The opponent remains troubled by the notion of evaluating human worth, but finally admits that he is willing to grant that the life of the innocent is worth somewhat more than that of the murderer. Yet he goes on to give his fundamental objection:

> O: The basic problem with your wager is simply that we have no reason to think that C.P. does work, and in the absence of such reason, the probability that it does is virtually zero. In general, your proponents seems confused about the evidence. First, you say C.P. deters. Then you are confronted with evidence such as: State A and State B have virtually identical capital crime rates but State A hasn't had C.P. for one hundred years. You reply, for instance, that this could be because State A has more Quakers, who are peaceloving folk and so help to keep the crime rate down. And, you say, with C.P and all those Quakers, State A perhaps could have had an even lower crime

rate. Since we do not know about all such variables, the evidence is "inconclusive." Here "inconclusive" can only mean that while the evidence does not indicate that C.P. deters, it also does not demonstrate that it does not.

The next thing we see is your proponents saying that we just do not know whether C.P. deters or not, since the evidence is "inconclusive." But for this to follow, "inconclusive" must mean something like "tends to point both ways." The only studies available, on your own account, fail to supply any evidence at all that it *does* deter. From this, we cannot get "inconclusive" in the latter sense; we can't say that "we just don't know" whether it deters, we can only conclude, "we have no reason to think it does." Its status as a deterrent is no different from, e.g., prolonged tickling of murderers' feet. It could deter, but why think it does? . . .

P: So you demand that we have definite, unequivocal evidence and very high probability that C.P. deters before it could be said to be justifiable.

O: No, I never said that . . . I think the "Best-Bet Argument" shows that the demand is too strong. Given the possible gains and losses, if there is even a strong possibility that it works, I do not think it would be irrational to give it another try. But we should do so in full cognizance of the betting situation. We would be taking lives on the chance that there will be more than compensating saving of lives. And, I also think that it is damned difficult to show that there is even a strong possibility that C.P. deters.[51]

There are several things to say about Conway's dialogue. Like his opponent, you may object that this kind of quantifying of human life is entirely inappropriate. But if you had to choose between saving an innocent person and saving one who had just committed cold-blooded murder, which would you choose? We generally judge that conscientiously moral people are more worthy than viciously immoral ones, that the innocent are more worthy of aid than those who are guilty of squandering aid. Van den Haag's argument only formalizes these comparisons and applies them to the practice of capital punishment. Some humans are worth more than others, and some have forfeited their right not to be killed, whereas most people have not. Our practices should take this into account.

Secondly, you may still have doubts about the validity of putting a value on human life. But ask yourself, "What gives humans value?" or "What gives their lives value?" From a religious perspective they may have intrinsic value, but they still may forfeit a right to life by committing murder.

---

51. David Conway, "Capital Punishment and Deterrence: Some Considerations in Dialogue Form," *Philosophy and Public Affairs* 3, no. 4 (Summer 1974).

But if you accept a secular point of view, isn't it some quality like moral integrity or contribution to the community that at least partly gives us worth? If so, then the murderer has lost a good bit of whatever value his life had. Kant, who set forth the idea that persons have intrinsic worth based on their ability to reason, held that we could forfeit that worth ("obliterate it") through immoral acts, so that the death penalty might well be appropriate.

Thirdly, if we had evidence that there was a 50 percent chance that executing a murderer would bring back the innocent victim, wouldn't you vote for the execution? I would vote for it if there was *virtually any chance* at all. But how different is that bet from the one that says there is a good chance that executing a person convicted of first-degree murder will prevent the murders of other innocent people? If the death penalty does deter, and we have evidence that it does, then we are partly responsible for the deaths of additional innocents by not inflicting that penalty.

Finally, the opponent is wrong in arguing that we have no evidence at all about the deterrent effect of capital punishment, so that it is tantamount to the evidence that tickling murderers' feet deters. We have evidence, though not statistical proof, based on commonsense experience, which makes the case for deterrence even stronger than the Best Bet argument. I now turn to the Argument from Anecdotal Evidence, a commonsense argument.

The Argument from Anecdotal Evidence

Abolitionists like Stephen Nathanson argue that because the statistical evidence in favor of the deterrent effect of capital punishment is indecisive, we have no basis for concluding that it is a better deterrent than long prison sentences.[52] If I understand these opponents, their argument presents us with an exclusive disjunct: Either we must have conclusive statistical evidence (i.e., a proof) for the deterrent effect of the death penalty, or we have no grounds for supposing that the death penalty deters. Many people accept this argument. Just this morning a colleague said to me, "There is no statistical evidence that the death penalty deters," as if to dismiss the argument from deterrence altogether. This is premature judgment, for the argument commits the fallacy of supposing that only two

---

52. Nathanson, *An Eye for an Eye?* Chap. 2.

opposites are possible. There is a middle position that holds that while we cannot prove conclusively that the death penalty deters, the weight of evidence supports its deterrence. Furthermore, I think there are too many variables to hold constant for us to prove via statistics the deterrence hypothesis, and even if the requisite statistics were available, we could question whether they were cases of mere correlation versus causation. On the other hand, commonsense or anecdotal evidence may provide insight into the psychology of human motivation, providing evidence that fear of the death penalty deters some types of would-be criminals from committing murder.[53] Granted, people are sometimes deceived about their motivation. But usually they are not deceived, and, as a rule, we should presume they know their motives until we have evidence to the contrary. The general commonsense argument goes like this:

1. What people (including potential criminals) fear more will have a greater deterrent effect on them.
2. People (including potential criminals) fear death more than they do any other humane punishment.
3. The death penalty is a humane punishment.
4. Therefore, people (including criminals) will be deterred more by the death penalty than by any other humane punishment.

Since the purpose of this argument is to show that the death penalty very likely deters more than long term prison sentences, I am assuming it is *humane*, that is, acceptable to the moral sensitivities of the majority in our society. Torture might deter even more, but it is not considered humane. I will say more about the significance of humaneness with regard to the death penalty below.

Common sense informs us that most people would prefer to remain out of jail, that the threat of public humiliation is enough to deter some people, that a sentence of twenty years will deter most people more than a sentence of two years, that a life sentence will deter most would-be crimi-

---

53. After I had written this section, Michael Davis sent me his article, "Death, Deterrence, and the Method of Common Sense," *Social Theory and Practice* 7, no. 2 (Summer 1981). He offers a similar commonsense argument for the deterrent effect of the death penalty. His article is especially useful in that it shows just how little the statistics of social science demonstrate and why we should take the commonsense data as weightier.

nals more than a sentence of twenty years. I think that we have common-sense evidence that the death penalty is a better deterrent than prison sentences. For one thing, as Richard Herrnstein and James Q. Wilson have argued in *Crime and Human Nature*, a great deal of crime is committed on a cost-benefit schema, wherein the criminal engages in some form of risk assessment as to his or her chances of getting caught and punished in some manner. If he or she estimates the punishment mild, the crime becomes inversely attractive, and vice versa. The fact that those who are condemned to death do everything in their power to get their sentences postponed or reduced to long-term prison sentences, in a way lifers do not, shows that they fear death more than life in prison.

The point is this: Imprisonment constitutes one evil, the loss of freedom, but the death penalty imposes a more severe loss, that of life itself. If you lock me up, I may work for a parole or pardon, I may learn to live stoically with diminished freedom, and I can plan for the day when my freedom has been restored. But if I believe that my crime may lead to death, or loss of freedom followed by death, then I have more to fear than mere imprisonment. I am faced with a great evil plus an even greater evil. I fear death more than imprisonment because it alone takes from me all future possibility.

I am not claiming that the fear of legal punishment is all that keeps us from criminal behavior. Moral character, habit, fear of being shamed, peer pressure, fear of authority, or the fear of divine retribution may have a greater influence on some people. However, many people will be deterred from crime, including murder, by the threat of severe punishment. The abolitionist points out that many would-be murderers simply do not believe they will be caught. Perhaps this is true for some. While the fantastic egoist has delusions of getting away with his crime, many would-be criminals are not so bold or delusionary.

Former Prosecuting Attorney for the State of Florida, Richard Gernstein has set forth the commonsense case for deterrence. First of all, he claims, the death penalty certainly deters the murderer from any further murders, including those he or she might commit within the prison where he is confined. Secondly, statistics cannot tell us how many potential criminals have refrained from taking another's life through fear of the death penalty. He quotes Judge Hyman Barshay of New York: "The death penalty is a warning, just like a lighthouse throwing its beams out to sea. We hear about shipwrecks, but we do not hear about the ships the lighthouse guides safely on their way. We do not have proof of the number of ships its saves, but we do not tear the lighthouse down."[54]

Some of the commonsense evidence is anecdotal as the following quotation shows. British member of Parliament Arthur Lewis explains how he was converted from an abolitionist to a supporter of the death penalty:

> One reason that has stuck in my mind, and which has proved [deterrence] to me beyond question, is that there was once a professional burglar in [my] constituency who consistently boasted of the fact that he had spent about one-third of his life in prison. . . . He said to me "I am a professional burglar. Before we go out on a job we plan it down to every detail. Before we go into the boozer to have a drink we say 'Don't forget, no shooters'—shooters being guns." He adds "We did our job and didn't have shooters because at that time there was capital punishment. Our wives, girlfriends and our mums said, 'Whatever you do, do not carry a shooter because if you are caught you might be topped [executed].' If you do away with capital punishment they will all be carrying shooters."[55]

It is difficult to know how widespread this reasoning is. My own experience corroborates this testimony. Growing up in the infamous Cicero, Illinois, home of Al Capone and the Mafia, I had friends who went into crime, mainly burglary and larceny. It was common knowledge that one stopped short of killing in the act of robbery. A prison sentence could be dealt with—especially with a good lawyer—but being convicted of murder, which at that time included a reasonable chance of being electrocuted, was an altogether different matter. No doubt exists in my mind that the threat of the electric chair saved the lives of some of those who were robbed in my town. No doubt some crimes are committed in the heat of passion or by the temporally (or permanently) insane, but some are committed through a process of risk assessment. Burglars, kidnappers, traitors and vindictive people will sometimes be restrained by the threat of death. We simply don't know how much capital punishment deters, but this sort of commonsense, anecdotal evidence must be taken into account in assessing the institution of capital punishment.

---

54. Richard E. Gernstein, "A Prosecutor Looks at Capital Punishment" *Journal of Criminal Law: Criminology and Police Science* 51, no. 2 (1960).

55. British *Parliamentary Debates* fifth series, vol. 23, issue 1243, House of Commons, 11 May 1982. Quoted in Tom Sorell, *Moral Theory and Capital Punishment* (Oxford: Blackwell, 1987), 36.

John Stuart Mill admitted that capital punishment does not inspire terror in hardened criminals, but it may well make an impression on prospective murderers. "As for what is called the failure of the death punishment, who is able to judge of that? We partly know who those are whom it has not deterred; but who is there who knows whom it has deterred, or how many human beings it has saved who would have lived to be murderers if that awful association had not been thrown round the idea of murder from their earliest infancy."[56] Mill's points are well taken: (1) Not everyone will be deterred by the death penalty, but some will; (2) The potential criminal need not consciously calculate a cost-benefit analysis regarding his crime to be deterred by the threat. The idea of the threat may have become a subconscious datum "from their earliest infancy." The repeated announcement and regular exercise of capital punishment may have deep causal influence.

Gernstein quotes the British Royal Commission on Capital Punishment (1949–53), which concluded that there was evidence that the death penalty has some deterrent effect on normal human beings. Some of its evidence in favor of the deterrence effect includes:

1. "Criminals who have committed an offense punishable by life imprisonment, when faced with capture, refrained from killing their captor though by killing, escape seemed probable. When asked why they refrained from the homicide, quick responses indicated a willingness to serve life sentence, but not risk the death penalty."
2. "Criminals about to commit certain offenses refrained from carrying deadly weapons. Upon apprehension, answers to questions concerning absence of such weapons indicated a desire to avoid more serious punishment by carrying a deadly weapon, and also to avoid use of the weapon which could result in imposition of the death penalty."
3. "Victims have been removed from a capital punishment state to a non-capital punishment state to allow the murderer opportunity for homicide without threat to his own life. This in itself demonstrates that the death penalty is considered by some would-be-killers."[57]

---

56. *Parliamentary Debates*, third series, April 21, 1868. Reprinted in Peter Singer, ed., *Applied Ethics* (Oxford University Press, 1986), 97–104.
57. Ibid.

Gernstein then quotes former District Attorney of New York, Frank S. Hogan, representing himself and his associates:

> We are satisfied from our experience that the deterrent effect is both real and substantial . . . for example, from time to time accomplices in felony murder state with apparent truthfulness that in the planning of the felony they strongly urged the killer not to resort to violence. From the context of these utterances, it is apparent that they were led to these warnings to the killer by fear of the death penalty which they realized might follow the taking of life. Moreover, victims of hold-ups have occasionally reported that one of the robbers expressed a desire to kill them and was dissuaded from so doing by a confederate. Once again, we think it not unreasonable to suggest that fear of the death penalty played a role in some of these intercessions.
>
> On a number of occasions, defendants being questioned in connection with homicide have shown a striking terror of the death penalty. While these persons have in fact perpetrated homicide, we think that their terror of the death penalty must be symptomatic of the attitude of many others of their type, as a result of which many lives have been spared.[58]

It seems likely that the death penalty does not deter as much as it could due to its inconsistent and rare use. For example, out of an estimated 23,370 cases of murder, nonnegligent manslaughter, and rape in 1949, there were only 119 executions carried out in the United States. In 1953, only 62 executions out of 7,000 cases for those crimes took place. Few executions were carried out in the 1960s and none at all from 1967 to 1977. Gernstein points out that at that rate a criminal's chances of escaping execution are better than 100 to 1. Actually, since Gernstein's report, the figures have become even more weighted against the chances of the death sentence. In 1993, there were 24,526 cases of murder and nonnegligent manslaughter and only 56 executions; and in 1994, there were 23,305 cases of murder and nonnegligent manslaughter and only 31 executions—for a ratio of better than 750 to 1 in favor of the criminal. The average length of stay for a prisoner executed in 1994 was ten years and two months. If potential murderers perceived the death penalty as a highly probable outcome of murder, would they not be more reluctant to kill? Gernstein notes:

> The commissioner of police of London, England, in his evidence before the Royal Commission on Capital Punishment, told of a gang of armed robbers

---

58. Quoted in Gernstein, "A Prosecutor Looks at Capital Punishment."

who continued operations after one of their members was sentenced to death
and his sentence commuted to penal servitude, but the same gang disbanded
and disappeared when, on a later occasion, two others were convicted of
murder and hanged.[59]

Gernstein sums up his data: "Surely it is a commonsense argument,
based on what is known of human nature, that the death penalty has a
deterrent effect particularly for certain kinds of murderers. Furthermore,
as the Royal Commission opined the death penalty helps to educate the
conscience of the whole community, and it arouses among many people a
quasi-religious sense of awe. In the mind of the public there remains a
strong association between murder and the penalty of death. Certainly one
of the factors which restrains some people from murder is fear of punishment and surely, since people fear death more than anything else, the
death penalty is the most effective deterrent."[60]

I should also point out that, given the retributivist argument for the
death penalty, based on desert, the retentionist does not have to prove
that the death penalty deters *better* than long prison sentences, but if the
death penalty is deemed at least as effective as its major alternative, it
would be justified. If evidence existed that life imprisonment were a *more
effective* deterrent, the retentionist might be hard pressed to defend it on
retributivist lines alone. My view is that the desert argument plus the commonsense evidence—being bolstered by the Best Bet Argument—strongly
supports retention of the death penalty.

It is noteworthy that prominent abolitionists, such as Charles Black,
Hugo Adam Bedau, Ramsey Clark, and Henry Schwartzchild, have admitted to Ernest van den Haag that even if every execution were to deter a
hundred murders, they would oppose it, from which van den Haag concludes "to these abolitionist leaders, the life of every murderer is more
valuable than the lives of a hundred prospective victims, for these abolitionists would spare the murderer, even if doing so will cost a hundred
future victims their lives." Black and Bedau said they would favor abolishing the death penalty even if they knew that doing so would increase the
homicide rate 1,000 percent.[61] This response of abolitionists is puzzling,

---

59. Ibid.
60. Ibid.
61. Cited in Ernest van den Haag, "The Death Penalty Once More, Unpublished manuscript: 18 available from van den Haag. In "A Response to Bedau"

since one of Bedau's arguments against the death penalty is that it doesn't bring back the dead. "We cannot do anything for the dead victims of crime. (How many of those who oppose the death penalty would continue to do so if, *mirabile dictu*, executing the murderer might bring the victim back to life?)"[62] Apparently, he would support the death penalty if it brought a dead victim back to life, but not if it prevented a hundred innocent victims from being murdered.

If the Best Bet Argument is sound, or if the death penalty does deter would-be murderers, as common sense suggests, then we should support some uses of the death penalty. It should be used for those who commit first-degree murder, for whom no mitigating factors are present, and especially for those who murder police officers, prison guards, and political leaders. Many states rightly favor it for those who murder while committing another crime, e.g., burglary or rape. It should also be used for treason and terrorist bombings.

The Golden Rule Argument

One more argument should be set forth, the Golden Rule Argument for the death penalty. The Golden Rule states that we should do unto others as we would have them do unto us. Reflect on the evil deeds perpetrated by those who blew up the Murrah Federal Building on Oklahoma City April 19, 1995, killing 168 people or reread the descriptions of heinous murders discussed by Mike Royko at the beginning of this part of this essay. If you had yielded to temptation and blown up the Murrah Federal Building or if you, like Steven Judy, had raped and murdered a helpless woman and then drowned her three small children,—or if you had kidnapped a young girl, placed her in your trunk, and then killed her, what punishment do you think would be fitting for *you?* What would you deserve? Would you want to live? Would not the *moral* guilt that you

---

(*Arizona State Law Journal* 4 [1977]) van den Haag states that both Black and Bedau said that they would be in favor of abolishing the death penalty even if "they knew that its abolition (and replacement by life imprisonment) would increase the homicide rate by 10%, 20%, 50%, 100%, or 1000%. Both gentlemen continued to answer affirmatively." Bedau confirmed this in a letter to me (July 28, 1996).

62. Hugo Adam Bedau, "How to Argue about the Death Penalty," in *Facing the Death Penalty*, ed. Michael Radelet (Temple University Press, 1989), 190.

would doubtless feel demand the death penalty? And would you not judge that such moral guilt was appropriate, so that anyone who did not feel it was morally defective? Would you not agree that you forfeited your right to life, that you had brought upon yourself the hangman's noose? Would you not agree that you *deserved* nothing less than death? Should we not apply these sentiments to murderers? Should we not apply the Golden Rule to those who do heinous evil? Are not some crimes so evil that the very stones cry out for retribution?

Objections to Capital Punishment

Let us examine six of the major objections to capital punishment, as well as the retentionist's responses to those objections.

1. *Objection*: Capital punishment is a morally unacceptable thirst for revenge. As former British Prime Minister Edward Heath put it,

> The real point which is emphasized to me by many constituents is that even if the death penalty is not a deterrent, murderers deserve to die. This is the question of revenge. Again, this will be a matter of moral judgment for each of us. I do not believe in revenge. If I were to become the victim of terrorists, I would not wish them to be hanged or killed in any other way for revenge. All that would do is deepen the bitterness which already tragically exists in the conflicts we experience in society, particularly in Northern Ireland.[63]

Response: Retributivism, as we argued in Part I, is not the same thing as revenge, although the two attitudes are often intermixed in practice. Revenge is a personal response to a perpetrator for an injury. Retribution is an impartial and impersonal response to an offender for an offense done against someone. You cannot desire revenge for the harm of someone to whom you are indifferent. Revenge always involves personal concern for the victim. Retribution is not personal but based on objective factors: the criminal has deliberately harmed an innocent party and so *deserves* to be punished, whether I wish it or not. I would agree that I or my son or daughter *deserves* to be punished for our crimes, but I don't wish any vengeance on myself or my son or daughter.

Furthermore, while revenge often leads us to exact more suffering from

---

63. British *Parliamentary Debates*, 1982, quoted in Sorrell, *Moral Theory*, 43.

the offender than the offense warrants, retribution stipulates that the offender be punished in proportion to the gravity of the offense. In this sense, the *lex talionis* which we find in the Old Testament is actually a progressive rule, where retribution replaces revenge as the mode of punishment. It says that there are limits to what one may do to the offender. Revenge demands a life for an eye or a tooth, but Moses provides a rule that exacts a penalty equal to the harm done by the offender.

2. *Objection:* Perhaps the murderer does deserve to die, but by what authority does the state execute him or her? Both the Old and New Testament says, " 'Vengeance is mine, I will repay,' says the Lord" (Prov. 25:21 and Romans 12:19). You need special authority to justify taking the life of a human being.[64]

Response: The objector fails to note that the New Testament passage continues with a support of the right of the state to execute criminals in the name of God: "Let every person be subjected to the governing authorities. For there is no authority except from God, and those that exist have been instituted by God. Therefore he who resists what God has appointed, and those who resist will incur judgment. . . . If you do wrong, be afraid, for [the authority] does not bear the sword in vain; he is the servant of God to execute his wrath on the wrongdoer" (Romans 13:1–4). So, according to the Bible, the authority to punish, which presumably includes the death penalty, comes from God.

But we need not appeal to a religious justification for capital punishment. We can site the state's role in dispensing justice. Just as the state has the authority (and duty) to act justly in allocating scarce resources, in meeting minimal needs of its (deserving) citizens, in defending its citizens from violence and crime, and in not waging unjust wars; so too does it have the authority, flowing from its mission to promote justice and the good of its people, to punish the criminal. If the criminal, as one who has forfeited a right to life, deserves to be executed, especially if it will likely deter would-be murderers, the state has a duty to execute those convicted of first-degree murder.

3. *Objection:* Miscarriages of justice occur. Capital punishment is to be rejected because of human fallibility in convicting innocent parties and sentencing them to death. In a survey done in 1985 Hugo Adam Bedau

---

64. Both Stephen Nathanson (in a letter of November 1996) and John Kleinig (in conversation) have raised this objection.

and Michael Radelet found that of the 7,000 persons executed in the
United States between 1900 and 1985, 25 were innocent of capital
crimes.[65] While some compensation is available to those unjustly impris-
oned, the death sentence is irrevocable. We can't compensate the dead. As
John Maxton, a member of the British Parliament puts it, "If we allow
one innocent person to be executed, morally we are committing the same,
or, in some ways, a worse crime than the person who committed the
murder."[66]

Response: Mr. Maxton is incorrect in saying that mistaken judicial execution is morally the same or worse than murder, for a deliberate intention
to kill the innocent occurs in a murder, whereas no such intention occurs
in wrongful capital punishment.

Sometimes this objection is framed this way: It is better to let ten criminals go free than to execute one innocent person. If this dictum is a call
for safeguards, then it is well taken; but somewhere there seems to be
a limit on the tolerance of society towards capital offenses. Would these
abolitionists argue that it is better that 50 or 100 or 1,000 murderers go
free than that one guilty person be executed? Society has a right to protect
itself from capital offenses even if this means taking a finite chance of executing an innocent person. If the basic activity or process is justified, then
it is regrettable, but morally acceptable, that some mistakes are made. Fire
trucks occasionally kill innocent pedestrians while racing to fires, but we
accept these losses as justified by the greater good of the activity of using
fire trucks. We judge the use of automobiles to be acceptable even though
such use causes an average of 50,000 traffic fatalities each year. We accept
the morality of a defensive war even though it will result in our troops
accidentally or mistakenly killing innocent people.

The fact that we can err in applying the death penalty should give us
pause and cause us to build an appeals process into the judicial system.
Such a process is already in the American and British legal systems. That
occasional error may be made, regrettable though this is, is not a sufficient
reason for us to refuse to use the death penalty, if on balance it serves a
just and useful function.

---

65. Hugo Adam Bedau and Michael Radelet, *Miscarriages of Justice in Potential Capital Cases* (1st draft Oct. 1985, on file at Harvard Law School Library),
quoted in E. van den Haag "The Ultimate Punishment: A Defense," *Harvard
Law Review* 99, no. 7 (May 1986): 1664.

66. Ibid., 47.

Furthermore, abolitionists are simply misguided in thinking that prison sentences are a satisfactory alternative here. It's not clear that we can always or typically compensate innocent parties who waste away in prison. Jacques Barzun has argued that a prison sentence can be worse than death and carries all the problems that the death penalty does regarding the impossibility of compensation:

> In the preface of his useful volume of cases, *Hanged in Error*, Mr. Leslie Hale refers to the tardy recognition of a minor miscarriage of justice—one year in jail: "The prisoner emerged to find that his wife had died and that his children and his aged parents had been removed to the workhouse. By the time a small payment had been assessed as 'compensation' the victim was incurably insane." So far we are as indignant with the law as Mr. Hale. But what comes next? He cites the famous Evans case, in which it is very probable that the wrong man was hanged, and he exclaims: "While such mistakes are possible, should society impose an irrevocable sentence?" Does Mr. Hale really ask us to believe that the sentence passed on the first man, whose wife died and who went insane, was in any sense *revocable?* Would not any man rather be Evans dead than that other wretch "emerging" with his small compensation and his reason for living gone?[67]

The abolitionist is incorrect in arguing that death is different than long-term prison sentences because it is irrevocable. Imprisonment also take good things away from us that may never be returned. We cannot restore to the inmate the freedom or opportunities he or she lost. Suppose an innocent 25-year-old man is given a life sentence for murder. Thirty years later the mistake is discovered and he is set free. Suppose he values three years of freedom to every one year of prison life. That is, he would rather live ten years as a free man than thirty as a prisoner. Given this man's values, the criminal justice system has taken the equivalent of ten years of life from him. If he lives until he is 65, he has, as far as his estimation is concerned, lost ten years, so that he may be said to have lived only 55 years.[68]

The numbers in this example are arbitrary, but the basic point is sound.

---

67. Jacques Barzun, "In Favor of Capital Punishment," *The American Scholar* 31, no. 2 (Spring 1962)

68. I have been influenced by similar arguments by Michael Levin (unpublished manuscript) and Michael Davis, "Is the Death Penalty Irrevocable?" *Social Theory and Practice* 10, no. 2 (Summer 1984).

Most of us would prefer a shorter life of higher quality to a longer one of low quality. Death prevents all subsequent quality, but imprisonment also irrevocably harms one in diminishing the quality of life of the prisoner.

4. *Objection*: The death penalty is unjust because it discriminates against the poor and minorities, particularly, African Americans, over rich people and whites. Former Supreme Court Justice William Douglas wrote that "a law which reaches that [discriminatory] result in practice has no more sanctity than a law which in terms provides the same."[69] Nathanson argues that "in many cases, whether one is treated justly or not depends not only on what one deserves but on how other people are treated."[70] He offers the example of unequal justice in a plagiarism case. "I tell the students in my class that anyone who plagiarizes will fail the course. Three students plagiarize papers, but I give only one a failing grade. The other two, in describing their motivation, win my sympathy, and I give them passing grades." Arguing that this is patently unjust, he likens this case to the imposition of the death penalty and concludes that it too is unjust.

Response: First of all, it is not true that a law that is applied in a discriminatory manner is unjust. Unequal justice is no less justice, however uneven its application. The discriminatory application, not the law itself, is unjust. A just law is still just even if it is not applied consistently. For example, a friend of mine once got two speeding tickets during a 100-mile trip (having borrowed my car). He complained to the police officer who gave him his second ticket that many drivers were driving faster than he was at the time. They had escaped detection, he argued, so it wasn't fair for him to get two tickets on one trip. The officer acknowledged the imperfections of the system but, justifiably, had no qualms about giving him the second ticket. Unequal justice is still justice, however regrettable. So Justice Douglas is wrong in asserting that discriminatory results invalidate the law itself. The discriminatory practice should be reformed, and in many cases it can be. But imperfect practices in themselves do not entail that the laws engendering these practices are themselves are unjust.

With regard to Nathanson's analogy with the plagiarism case, two things should be said against it. First, if the teacher is convinced that the motivational factors are mitigating factors, then he or she may be justified

---

69. Justice William Douglas in *Furman v Georgia* 408 U.S. 238 (1972).
70. Nathanson, *An Eye for an Eye?*, 62.

in passing two of the plagiarizing students. Suppose that the one student did no work whatsoever, showed no interest (Nathanson's motivation factor) in learning, and exhibited no remorse in cheating, whereas the other two spent long hours seriously studying the material and, upon apprehension, showed genuine remorse for their misdeeds. To be sure, they yielded to temptation at certain—though limited—sections of their long papers, but the vast majority of their papers represented their own diligent work. Suppose, as well, that all three had C averages at this point. The teacher gives the unremorseful, gross plagiarizer an F but relents and gives the other two D's. Her actions parallel the judge's use of mitigating circumstances and cannot be construed as arbitrary, let alone unjust.

The second problem with Nathanson's analogy is that it would have disastrous consequences for all law and benevolent practices alike. If we concluded that we should abolish a rule or practice, unless we treated everyone exactly by the same rules all the time, we would have to abolish, for example, traffic laws and laws against imprisonment for rape, theft, and even murder. Carried to its logical limits, we would also have to refrain from saving drowning victims if a number of people were drowning but we could only save a few of them. Imperfect justice is the best that we humans can attain. We should reform our practices as much as possible to eradicate unjust discrimination wherever we can, but if we are not allowed to have a law without perfect application, we will be forced to have no laws at all.

Nathanson acknowledges this latter response but argues that the case of death is different. "Because of its finality and extreme severity of the death penalty, we need to be more scrupulous in applying it as punishment than is necessary with any other punishment."[71] The retentionist agrees that the death penalty is a severe punishment and that we need to be scrupulous in applying it. The difference between the abolitionist and the retentionist seems to lie in whether we are wise and committed enough as a nation to reform our institutions so that they approximate fairness. Apparently, Nathanson is pessimistic here, whereas I have faith in our ability to learn from our mistakes and reform our systems. If we can't reform our legal system, what hope is there for us?

More specifically, the charge that a higher percentage of blacks than whites are executed was once true but is no longer so. Many states have

---

71. Ibid., 67.

made significant changes in sentencing procedures, with the result that currently whites convicted of first-degree murder are sentenced to death at a higher rate than blacks.[72]

One must be careful in reading too much into these statistics. While great disparities in statistics should cause us to examine our judicial procedures, they do not in themselves prove injustice. For example, more males than females are convicted of violent crimes (almost 90% of those convicted of violent crimes are males—a virtually universal statistic), but this is not strong evidence that the law is unfair, for there are psychological explanations for the disparity in convictions. Males are on average and by nature more aggressive (usually tied to testosterone) than females. Likewise, there may be good explanations why people of one ethnic group commit more crimes than those of other groups, explanations which do not impugn the processes of the judicial system.[73]

5. *Objection:* The Minimal Harm Argument against the death penalty. As I was preparing this essay, Hugo Adam Bedau sent me a paper attacking the death penalty on the grounds that "[S]ociety (acting through the authority of its government) must not use laws that impose more restrictive—violent, harmful, invasive—interference with human liberty than is necessary as a means to achieve legitimate social objectives."[74] Bedau ar-

---

72. The Department of Justice's *Bureau of Justice Statistics Bulletin* for 1994 reports that between 1977 and 1994, 2,336 (51%) of those arrested for murder were white, 1,838 (40%) were black, 316 (7%) were Hispanic. Of the 257 who were executed, 140 (54%) were white, 98 (38%) were black, 17 (7%) were Hispanic and 2 (1%) were other races. In 1994, 31 prisoners, 20 white men and 11 black men, were executed although whites made up only 7,532 (41%) and blacks 9,906 (56%) of those arrested for murder. Of those sentenced to death in 1994, 158 were white men, 133 were black men, 25 were Hispanic men, 2 were Native American men, 2 were white women, and 3 were black women. Of those sentenced, relatively more blacks (72%) than whites (65%) or Hispanics (60%) had prior felony records. Overall the criminal justice system does not seem to favor white criminals over black, though it does seem to favor rich defendants over poor ones.

73. For instance, according to FBI figures for 1992, the U.S. murder rate was 9.3, far higher than that of France (4.5), Germany (3.9) or Austria (3.9). Of the 23,760 murders committed in the United States that year, 55% of the offenders whose race was known were black and 43% white. Since blacks compose 12.1% of the U.S. population, the murder rate for blacks in 1992 was 45 per 100,000, while that for whites was 4.78—a figure much closer to that for European whites.

74. From Hugo Adam Bedau, "Moral Arguments and the Death Penalty: Is Absolute Abolition a Tenable Policy?" delivered at the Annual Meeting of the American Philosophical Association, 28 December 1996.

gues that the death penalty is never necessary to achieve valid social objectives, because "some other form of legitimate deprivation, such as the deprivation of liberty by means of long-term imprisonment, is sufficient." He cites as evidence that abolitionist jurisdictions such as Michigan, Wisconsin, Minnesota and Rhode Island have no worse crime records than states with the death penalty, such as Illinois. So, it seems to follow, the minimal harm argument urges us to abolish the death penalty in all states.

Response: First, Bedau seems to have neglected some vital statistics. Although the murder rates for Illinois and Michigan are similar, one should take into consideration urban areas where crime is rampant. For example, Detroit, Michigan has one of the highest crime rates in the nation, far higher than the much larger city of Chicago, Illinois. Detroit's homicide rate among juveniles grew from 8 per 100,000 to 30 per 100,000 during the course of the 1980s. Regarding the lower-than-average rates in Wisconsin and Minnesota, other factors besides the presence or absence of the death penalty could explain differences in homicide rates in these states. Bedau needs to take into account the general arguments for deterrence, as well as the fact that the death penalty is seldom carried out (31 executions in 1994). If the arguments Ehrlich, van den Haag, and others have set forth for the deterrent effect of the death penalty are correct, we could accept Bedau's general (do minimal harm) thesis and still advocate the death penalty.

Second, there is a retributive consideration to be brought into the argument. We—the state, using due process—should execute the murderer because he deserves it. The state has a prima facie obligation to give people what they deserve. Even as it has a duty to meet the needs of the deserving poor—by helping to create jobs, providing unemployment insurance and welfare—so it has a prima facie duty to punish those who do evil things to fellow citizens. In other words, one of the purposes of the state is retributive—both positive and negative. And of course the duty is prima facie. If the state doesn't have the means to do these things, or if mitigating circumstances exist, including the appropriateness of mercy to first offenders, then the duty may be overridden.

Note that an ancient tradition going as far back as the Book of Genesis holds that even in the state of nature murderers deserve death, so that anyone who finds a murderer has a duty to execute him. Recall that the first murderer, Cain, who slew his brother, complained, "Behold, thou hast driven me this day from the ground and whoever finds me will slay me" (Genesis 4:14). In forming the state we give up our right to carry out the moral law, entrusting this prerogative to the state.

6. *Objection:* The death penalty is a "cruel and unusual punishment." The death penalty constitutes a denial of the wrongdoer's essential dignity as a human being. No matter how bad a person becomes, no matter how terrible one's deed, we must never cease to regard a person as an end in himself or herself, as someone with inherent dignity. Capital punishment violates that dignity. As such it violates the Constitution of the United States of America, which forbids "cruel and unusual" punishments. Here is how Justice Thurgood Marshall stated it in *Gregg v Georgia:*

> To be sustained under the Eighth Amendment, the death penalty must [comport] with the basic concept of human dignity at the core of the Amendment; the objective in imposing it must be [consistent] with our respect for the dignity of [other] men. Under these standards, the taking of life "because the wrongdoer deserves it" surely must fail, for such a punishment has as its very basis the total denial of the wrongdoer's dignity and worth. The death penalty, unnecessary to promote the goal of deterrence or to further any legitimate notion of retribution, is an excessive penalty forbidden by the Eighth and Fourteenth Amendments.[75]

Similarly, in *Furman v Georgia* (1972) Justice William Brennan condemned capital punishment because it treats "members of the human race as nonhumans, as objects to be toyed with and discarded," adding that it is "inconsistent with the fundamental premise of the Clause that even the vilest criminal remains a human being possessed of common human dignity."[76]

Response: First of all, Justice Marshall differs with the framers of the Constitution about the meaning of "cruel and unusual" in declaring that the death penalty violates the Eighth Amendment's prohibition against "cruel and unusual" punishments—unless one would accuse the framers of the Constitution of contradicting themselves; for the Fifth and Fourteenth Amendments clearly authorize the death penalty.[77] The phrase

---

75. Justice Thurgood Marshall, *Gregg v Georgia* (1976).

76. Justice William Brennan, *Furman v Georgia* (1972).

77. The Fifth Amendment permits depriving people of "life, liberty or property," if the deprivation occurs with "due process of law," and the Fourteenth Amendment applies this provision to the states, "no State shall . . . deprive any person of life, liberty, or property, without due process of law."

"cruel and unusual" in the Eighth Amendment seems to mean cruel and *uncustomary or new* punishments, for, as van den Haag notes, "the framers did not want judges to invent *new* cruel punishments, but did not abolish customary ones."[78] But even if the framers did intend to prohibit the death penalty, I would argue that it is morally justified. The law is not always identical to what is morally correct.

Rather than being a violation of the wrongdoer's dignity, capital punishment may constitute a recognition of human dignity. As we noted in discussing Kant's view of retribution, the use of capital punishment respects the worth of the victim in calling for an equal punishment to be exacted from the offender, and it respects the dignity of the offender in treating him or her as a free agent who must be respected for his or her decisions and who must bear the cost of his or her acts as a responsible agent.

Let's look at these two points a bit more closely. The first—that capital punishment respects the worth of the victim—is bluntly articulated by the newspaper columnist, Mike Royko:

> When I think of the thousands of inhabitants of Death Rows in the hundreds of prisons in this country, I don't react the way the kindly souls do—with revulsion that the state would take these lives. My reaction is: What's taking us so long? Let's get that electrical current flowing. Drop the pellets now!
> Whenever I argue this with friends who have opposite views, they say that I don't have enough regard for that most marvelous of miracles—human life.
> Just the opposite: It's because I have so much regard for human life that I favor capital punishment. Murder is the most terrible crime there is. Anything less than the death penalty is an insult to the victim and society. It says, in effect, that we don't value the victim's life enough to punish the killer fully.[79]

It is precisely because the victim's life is sacred that the death penalty is sometimes the only fitting punishment for first-degree murder. I am accepting here the idea that there is something "sacred" or "dignified" about human life, though earlier I gave reasons which should cause secularists to doubt this.

Secondly, it's precisely because the murderer is an autonomous, free

---

78. Ernest van den Haag, "Why Capital Punishment?" *Albany Law Review* 54 (1990).

79. Mike Royko, *Chicago Sun-Times* (September 1983).

agent that we regard his or her act of murder as his own and hold him responsible for it. Not to hold the murderer responsible for his crime is to treat him as less than autonomous. Just as we praise and reward people in proportion to the merit of their good deeds, so we blame and punish them in proportion to the evil of their bad deeds. If there is evidence that the offender did not act freely, we would mitigate his sentence. But if the offender did act of his own free will, he bears the responsibility for those actions and deserves to be punished accordingly.

Of course, there are counter-responses to all of the retentionist's responses. Consider the utilitarian matter of cost. The appeals process, which is necessary to our system of justice, is so prolonged and expensive that it might not be worth the costs simply to satisfy our sense of retribution. Furthermore, most moderate retributivists do not argue that there is an *absolute* duty to execute first-degree murderers. Even the principle that the guilty should suffer in proportion to the harm they caused is not absolute. It can be overridden by mercy. But such mercy must be judicious, serving the public good.

In the same vein many argue that life imprisonment without parole will accomplish just as much as the death penalty. The retentionist would respond that death is a more fitting punishment for one who kills in cold blood, and utilitarians (deterrentists) would be concerned about the possibility of escape, murders committed by the murderer while incarcerated, and the enormous costs of keeping a prisoner incarcerated for life. Imprisonment without parole, advocated by many abolitionists as an alternative to the death penalty, should be given serious consideration in special cases, as when there is evidence that the murderer has suitably repented. But even in these cases the desert argument and the Best Bet argument would lean towards the death penalty.

No doubt we should work toward the day when capital punishment is no longer necessary, when the murder rate becomes a tiny fraction of what it is today, when a civilized society can safely incarcerate the few violent criminals in its midst, and where moral reform of the criminal is a reality. Perhaps this is why several European nations have abolished it (e.g., the murder rate in Detroit alone is 732 times that of the nation of Austria). I for one regret the use of the death penalty. I would vote for its abolition in an instant if only one condition were met: that those contemplating murder would set an example for me. Otherwise, it is better that the murderer perish than that innocent victims be cut down by the murderer's knife or bullet.

Is the Abolitionist Consistent?

Finally, I want to challenge the consistency of abolitionists who oppose capital punishment but support abortion. Former Supreme Court Justice William Brennan opposed the death penalty as "uniquely degrading to human dignity," but he had no trouble supporting abortion. I find this puzzling, in some cases entirely hypocritical. For abolitionists so stridently to oppose the death penalty for vicious murderers, who deserve death, and to support abortion of human fetuses, who are completely innocent of any wrong-doing, seems a glaring contradiction. Such is the Humpty Dumpty moral madness of our day that we condone the murder each year of two million human beings (from a biological classification at any rate), too helpless to defend themselves, and become apoplectic over the execution of an average of 65 cold-blooded murderers. "Protection for the Murderer—Death to the Innocent!" seems the implicit motto of the abolitionist who supports abortion.

I can understand how one can regretfully support abortion, as I do, since the fetus is not a full person and since utilitarian arguments may lead us to conclude that it is better for society not to produce unwanted and/or deformed children. But if we accept these arguments, then it would seem we should, even regretfully, accept the desert and deterrent arguments for the death penalty. If it is not unjust to kill, even to cause great suffering, in an innocent fetus on the way to full personhood in the third trimester, is it unjust to execute someone who has with malice aforethought murdered another human being, especially when there is evidence that this execution will deter others from murdering?

I recognize that those who hold a pro-choice position will object that I am missing the point: that fetuses are not *persons*, so they have no right not to be killed. Given the secularist's assumption that persons are made by socialization, I can understand the conclusion that fetuses are not persons (and of course neither are infants persons, but we inconsistently try people for murder in cases of infanticide), but I don't think the personhood argument can bear the weight alone. The fetus progressively nears personhood, has all the physiological organization necessary to activate self-consciousness, and has a high probability of doing so. Women opt to kill their fetuses because of the threat or likelihood of personal suffering or inconvenience. They do so for valid self-interested or utilitarian reasons. Yet the fetuses are innocent of any crime. Should the state not be allowed to do to murderers what mothers are allowed to do to innocent fetuses? And for the same reasons (utility) and better reasons (desert)? The murderers, at least, deserve to be executed.

Conclusion

Both abolitionists and retributivists agree that punishment for crime is meant to deter (1) the criminal and (2) potential criminals from future crimes. In this way it is *future* oriented. But we could deter people from crimes by framing and punishing the innocent. That would violate justice. The innocent deserve better. So we must recognize the retributive core in punishment. It is a necessary condition that the person punished be guilty of the crime in question. He or she *deserves* the punishment. We also hold that the guilty *ought* to be punished (and punished to the degree of the gravity of the offense). That is, guilt is a *sufficient* condition for punishment (and punishment to the degree of the gravity of the offense). Of course, we are free to be merciful, to take mitigating circumstances into account, to punish the criminal less than he deserves. For example, we ought not rape the rapist or torture the torturer (though he deserves equivalent treatment), for desert is not an absolute value—only a strong prima facie one. Suppose that Charley, our murderer, tortures 35 people, rapes 17 of them and then burns all of his victims in boiling oil. Must we do all that to Charley? We can't kill him more than once (though I suppose we can resuscitate him every time his heart stops and begin the ghoulish process again). There are limits to the evil we should inflict on people—even though they may deserve more. The question is just where those limits lie. Here retributivists may reasonably differ among themselves, and some, the "mild retributivists," will argue that we should stop short of the death penalty.

I regard that as a mistake, for death is not necessarily a "cruel or unusual" punishment, but a fitting limit. The death penalty can be economically sound, cause minimal pain (not that we should complain about the criminal suffering some pain), express our condemnation of capital offenses, be deserved, and yet serve as an adequate deterrent—which long-term imprisonment does not do to the same degree. My argument is that it best meets the criteria of the two main theories of punishment: retribution and deterrence. True, it does not satisfy the mandates of the third theory of punishment, rehabilitation, as well as abolitionism does, but as we saw, rehabilitationism is intrinsically weak, so the fact that it is incompatible with capital punishment is not a good reason to reject capital punishment.

Here is the structure of the argument as I have presented it in this part of my essay :

1. There is no sound argument that prohibits all uses of capital punishment; that is, there are no good reasons to view capital punishment as necessarily wrong.
2. The best grounds for abolitionism is the idea of essential human positive worth, which entails that we treat humans with special dignity. But a religious interpretation of this doctrine also prescribes a duty to punish those who with free will destroy the life of another human, and a secular interpretation of human dignity can only be based on moral status and function, so that when criminals fail these tests they forfeit their dignity, their right to life.
3. There is a sound retributive argument from desert for the thesis that capital punishment is a prima facie duty for capital offenses. This is confirmed via the Golden Rule Argument.
4. There is no sound argument that enjoins capital punishment for all cases of first degree murder.
5. There is also a secondary argument based on deterrence—in the form both of anecdotal, commonsense evidence and the Best-Bet Argument—that urges the use of capital punishment.
6. Therefore, since no abolitionist objection to capital punishment succeeds, and since two strong prima facie arguments for capital punishment exist, the burden of proof shifts to the abolitionist to provide grounds for why a duty to execute cold-blooded murderers should be overridden by other penalties.

Conclusion: Until the positive arguments for capital punishment are defeated, reason urges us to accept its legitimacy and work for fairness in its application.

Contrary to hard retributivists like Kant, I hold that there is no absolute necessity to resort to the death penalty. My argument is that, absent mitigating circumstances, the person who murders in cold blood (that is, with mens rea) deserves the death penalty. Sometimes mercy or a lesser penalty should be applied because of the difficulty in realizing equal justice, or because juries will not convict people if they think they will be sending them to their death, or because of the likelihood of executing an innocent person. These problems must be taken into account, but they do not offset the inherent justice of the death penalty for those who murder in cold blood. Eventually, we may find a better way to deal with criminals than we now have, which will produce a better—more moral—society. But even then, the murderer will deserve the death penalty.

2

Why the Death Penalty Should Be Abolished in America

Jeffrey Reiman

> *It is a fault to punish a fault in full.*
>
> Seneca, *On Clemency*

Death penalty advocates commonly press two claims in favor of executing murderers. The first is that the death penalty is a just punishment for murder, a murderer's just deserts. On this line of thought, we do injustice to the victims of murder if we do not execute their murderers. The second claim is that the death penalty is necessary to deter potential murderers. Here, the suggestion is that we do injustice to potential victims of murder if we do not execute actual ones. I accept that the death penalty is a just punishment for some murders—some murderers' just deserts—and that, if the death penalty were needed to deter future murders, it would be unjust to future victims not to impose it.[1] Notice, then, that I accept two of the strongest points urged in favor of the death penalty. If, granting these strong points, I can show that it would still be wrong to impose the death penalty, that should be a strong argument indeed. I shall argue for the following propositions:

---

1. It might be thought that we cannot *do* injustice by our *inaction*, and thus that this should rather say that we *allow* injustice by failing to punish murderers. However, the "we" in this phrase refers to us acting through the state, and I take the state to have (in part because it claims a monopoly on the right to punish criminals) a positive obligation to prevent grave injustice to its citizens. Then, when the state *allows* injustice to its citizens, it *does* them injustice.

1. that, though the death penalty is a just punishment for some murders, it is not unjust to punish murderers less harshly (down to a certain limit);
2. that, though the death penalty would be justified if needed to deter future murders, we have no good reason to believe that it is needed to deter future murders; and
3. that, in refraining from imposing the death penalty, the state, by its vivid and impressive example, contributes to reducing our tolerance for cruelty and thereby fosters the advance of human civilization as we understand it.

Taken together, these three propositions imply that we do no injustice to actual or potential murder victims, and we do some considerable good, in refraining from executing murderers. This conclusion will be reinforced by another argument, this one for the proposition

4. that, though the death penalty is *in principle* a just penalty for murder, it is unjust *in practice* in America because it is applied in arbitrary and discriminatory ways, and this is likely to continue into the foreseeable future.

This fourth proposition conjoined with the prior three imply the overall conclusion *that it is good in principle to avoid the death penalty and bad in practice to impose it.*

I shall proceed as follows. In section I, "Justifying Punishing," I consider the three main ways—retribution, fairness, and deterrence—in which punishment is thought morally justified, and I shall show how they can all be boiled down to one: *just desert.* In section II, "Death and Desert," I argue that the death penalty is just punishment for some murders, justly deserved by some murderers, but that it is not unjust to punish less harshly (down to a certain limit). In section III, "Death and Deterrence," I argue that the death penalty is not needed to deter future murderers, and thus we do no injustice by refraining from executing current murderers. In section IV, "Pain and Civilization," I defend the notion that punishing less harshly contributes to advancing human civilization as we understand it. In section V, "Just in Principle, Unjust in Practice," I indicate four ways in which the death penalty is administered unjustly in current-day

America and why it is likely to continue to be so.[2] The upshot of the first four sections is that it is *good in principle* to refrain from executing murderers, and the fifth section complements this conclusion by showing that executing murderers in America for the foreseeable future is likely to be *bad in practice*.

I. Justifying Punishing

Philosophers have tended to think that punishment can be justified in three distinct ways: *retribution*, that punishment is the offender's justly deserved payback for the harm he or she has caused; *fairness*, that punishment is a way of maintaining a fair distribution of civic burdens by imposing a burden on one who has shirked the burden of complying with the law; and *deterrence*, that punishment is an evil necessary to prevent greater future evils by giving potential criminals a disincentive to commit offenses.[3]

---

2. Sections II, III, and IV are based upon and substantially revise my "Justice, Civilization, and the Death Penalty: Answering van den Haag," *Philosophy and Public Affairs* 14, no. 2 (Spring 1985): 115–48. And section V is based upon and substantially revises my "The Justice of the Death Penalty in an Unjust World," in *Challenging Capital Punishment: Legal and Social Science Approaches*, ed. K. Haas & J. Inciardi (Beverly Hills, CA: Sage, 1988), 29–48.

3. Two other justifications for punishment are sometimes considered, namely, *incapacitation* (locking criminals up to protect us from their future crimes) and *moral education* (punishing to teach criminals the wrongness of what they did). Since incapacitation is aimed at preventing future crimes, I think it will be subject to the same considerations that pertain to the use of punishment for deterrence. The moral education approach stems from the laudable Platonic counsel that we should do no harm to anyone, and thus even punishment should be aimed at improving the offender. This approach suffers, I think, from three fatal flaws. First, there isn't evidence that many offenders don't know the wrongness of what they did. Second, if offenders really didn't know the wrongness of what they did, then they would not meet the requirements for moral responsibility and would better be treated as insufficiently rational or too immature to be held culpable. Third, if moral education is the justifying aim of punishment then it is doubtful that we are justified in punishing criminals who truly recognize the wrongness of their crimes before their sentences begin. Likewise, it would seem justified (perhaps even required) that we extend the sentences of those who have not learned the wrongness of what they did within the terms of their original sentences. Thus the moral education approach will tend in the direction of indeterminate sentencing, which

Each of these ways of justifying punishment will normally indicate different amounts of justified punishment. This may not seem troubling at first sight, since we might, as philosophers often do, opt for one rationale for punishment as the only really defensible one. But this is sure to result in counterintuitive outcomes for the same reasons that make the other two rationales plausible. I think that most people normally expect punishments to satisfy all three of the rationales for punishment. Thus, if the philosophical justification of punishment is to stay anywhere near the real world, we will have to show that all three rationales have a role to play in the determination of just punishment. And this does pose a problem, because philosophers have also argued that these punishment rationales are not compatible. For example, Immanuel Kant, the strictest of philosophical defenders of retribution, held that to punish someone for the purpose of deterrence is to use the person punished as a tool, a mere means, and thus to do him injustice.[4] However, if we punish only enough to give the offender his just retribution and not enough to deter future offenders, we seem to do injustice to potential victims.

Consequently, if the philosophical justification of punishment is to stay close to people's intuitions, we will have to show that such assertions of incompatibility are false, that the three rationales are not only compatible, but that their different prescriptions can be combined into a unitary mea-

---

shows, I think, the totalitarian tendency of any punishment regime that claims to do good for the criminal. Having said this much, I should add that my own view of the point of retributive punishment includes the idea that such punishment makes a statement to the criminal about his equality with his victim, and in this sense my view includes a certain amount of pedagogical content in punishment. Jean Hampton has striven to show that the moral education theory is "promising," though she admits that "[m]uch more work needs to be done before anyone is in a position to embrace the view wholeheartedly" (Jean Hampton, "The Moral Education Theory of Punishment," in *Punishment: A Philosophy and Public Affairs Reader*, ed. A. J. Simmons et al. [Princeton, NJ: Princeton University Press, 1995], 112–42; the quote is on 113).

4. Kant wrote that "[j]udicial punishment can never be used merely as a means to promote some other good for . . . civil society . . . ; for a human being can never be manipulated merely as a means to the purposes of someone else. . . . His innate personality protects him against such treatment." And further: "Only the Law of retribution (*jus talionis*) can determine exactly the kind and degree of punishment" (Immanuel Kant, "The Metaphysical Elements of Justice," pt. 1 of *The Metaphysics of Morals*, trans. J. Ladd [Indianapolis, IN: Bobbs-Merrill, 1965; originally published 1797], 100, 101).

sure of punishment capable of accomplishing the goal of each of the three without running afoul of either of the other two. I think that this can be done, but before turning to it, let us look at some arguments for the incompatibility of the three. This will give us a way to introduce the three rationales for punishment.

1. The Three Rationales for Punishment and Their Supposed Incompatibility

I shall speak at length about the retribution rationale and its various forms later. For the present, note that the retribution rationale normally takes its cue from the *lex talionis* ("an eye for an eye," and so on), which holds that the offender deserves harm equivalent to the harm he intentionally imposed (or attempted to impose)[5] on his victim. This doesn't mean that the punishment should duplicate the harm the criminal imposed, since that is often impossible. How, for example, could we duplicate the harm caused by a check forger or a spy? Rather, we are to find some penalty that (as near as we can judge) is equivalent to the harm caused, and (in our time) this will normally be some amount of time in prison (and sometimes death).[6]

Following Kant, I understand the *lex talionis* to take into account not only the harm caused by the criminal, but also the evil intention (called in the law *mens rea*) with which it is caused. Thus the punishment is to match criminals' evil, "in proportion to their inner viciousness" (to use Kant's phrase)[7] and in light of the harm viciously caused. It is because retributive

---

5. I shall not always repeat this qualification, but it should be taken as implied throughout.

6. Kant recognized that some crimes cannot be matched, either because it is impossible to do so, or because they are acts so evil that even when done to criminals who deserve them they "would themselves be punishable crimes against humanity in general" (Kant, "Metaphysical Elements of Justice," 132). Kant gives rape, pederasty, and bestiality as examples of such acts. Consequently, Kant allows—even goes on to suggest examples of—punishments that are equivalent to crimes without duplicating them. I do not, of course, mean to endorse Kant's specific proposals here.

7. Kant, "Metaphysical Elements of Justice," 103. Michael Davis agrees that "*lex talionis* includes both harm and fault in its calculation of deserved punishment" (Michael Davis, "Harm and Retribution," in *Punishment*, ed. Simmons et al., 198, see also 206).

punishment is for criminals' evil intention as well as for harm imposed that the *lex talionis* applies not only to completed crimes, but to attempts as well. In attempts, the evil intention is present and acted upon. Harm fails to occur only for reasons outside of the attempter's control.

Let us be clear about the relationship between *lex talionis* and retributivism. They are not the same. Retributivism—as the word itself suggests—is the doctrine that the offender should be *paid back* with suffering he deserves because of the evil he has intentionally done, and the *lex talionis* asserts that injury equivalent to what he intentionally imposed is what the offender deserves. In short, retribution refers to a class of punishment regimens that share the idea that punishment is justified as paying back the criminal with suffering that he deserves for the suffering he has caused. *Lex talionis* is a standard for measuring how much suffering is deserved. Thus we can speak of *lex talionis* as a version of retributivism, the version in which equivalence is the measure of deserved suffering.

Lex talionis is not the only version of retributivism. Another, which I shall call *proportional retributivism*, holds that what retribution requires is, not equivalence of harm between crimes and punishments, but "fit" or proportionality.[8] Our table of punishments should be organized ordinally so that it parallels the table of crimes. The worst crime will be punished by our worst punishment (even if less in harm than the crime), the second worst crime will be punished by our second worst punishment, and so on.[9] Note, here, that both this proportional form of retribution and the *lex talionis* form share the view that punishment is not to exceed the harm caused by the criminal. Either way, the *lex talionis* is the upper limit of punishment justified retributively. When I use the term "retribution," then, I mean a rationale for punishment that takes punishment to be justified as suffering deserved by the offender in light of the suffering he

---

8. Hugo Bedau writes: "'[R]etributive justice need not be thought to consist of *lex talionis*. One may reject that principle as too crude and still embrace the retributive principle that the severity of punishments should be graded according to the gravity of the offense" (Hugo A. Bedau, "Capital Punishment," in *Matters of Life and Death*, ed. Tom Regan [New York: Random House, 1980], 177). See also Andrew von Hirsch, "Doing Justice: The Principle of Commensurate Deserts," and Hyman Gross, "Proportional Punishment and Justifiable Sentences," both in *Sentencing*, ed. Hyman Gross and Andrew von Hirsch (New York: Oxford University Press, 1981), 243–56 and 272–83, respectively.

9. For a clear formulation of this notion, see Michael Davis,"How to Make the Punishment Fit the Crime," *Ethics* 93, no. 4 (July 1983): 736–41.

caused, where the measure of the suffering deserved is either equivalence or proportionality, but not more than equivalence.

Alan Goldman maintains that this feature of the retributivist approach to punishment is based on the idea that a criminal forfeits rights equivalent to the rights of her victim that she violates. Consequently, legitimate retributive punishment cannot be more than the harm caused by the crime. Goldman adds that, on this retributivist rationale, punishment that exceeds the harm caused by the criminal is undeserved in the same way as punishment of the innocent is undeserved. Since punishment of the innocent is a grave injustice, it follows that excessive punishment of the guilty is also a grave injustice—even if our anger for the criminal or our sympathy for her victim obscures this fact.

Goldman goes on to point out that the punishments we mete out, particularly for property crimes, seem clearly to be far harsher than the harms caused by the crimes themselves. Indeed, he contends that, if punishment is also to deter potential criminals, then it *must* be harsher than the harms that crimes normally cause. The reason for this is that, in our society, the chance of apprehension for most crimes is considerably below 50 percent. "Given these odds," Goldman writes, "a person pursuing what he considers his maximum prospective benefit may not be deterred by the threat of an imposition of punishment equivalent to the violation of the rights of the potential victim."[10] If criminals can anticipate being punished only half the time they commit crimes, then, to make it irrational for criminals to commit a crime, a penalty must represent a loss at least twice the gain that criminals expect from their crimes. Consequently, at least with property crimes (where the loss to the victim and the gain to the criminal are roughly the same), and possibly others, we will have to impose penalties greater than the harms that criminals have caused. Then, if we would punish justly according to the retributive rationale, we cannot deter future criminals, and if we would deter future criminals, we must punish unjustly. Observes Goldman,

> Caught in this dilemma, our society does not limit punishment to deprivation of [the criminal's] rights [equivalent to the] rights of others which have been violated by the criminal. Especially in regard to crimes against property, punishments by imprisonment are far more severe, on the average, than the

---

10. Alan H. Goldman, "The Paradox of Punishment," in *Punishment*, ed. Simmons et al., 36.

harm caused to victims of these crimes. Probably because such punishment is administered by officials of the state, cloaked in appropriate ritual and vested with authority, most of us systematically ignore its relative severity. If, however, we imagine an apolitical context, in which there is money and property, but no penal institution, would theft of several thousand dollars justify the victim's taking the perpetrator and locking him away in some small room for five to ten years?[11]

The justification of punishment by *fairness* was put forth by Herbert Morris in a now-classic article titled "Persons and Punishment." Morris writes:

> A person who violates the rules [that is, the laws of a just legal system] has something that others have—the benefits of the system—but by renouncing what others have assumed, the burdens of self-restraint, he has acquired an unfair advantage. Matters are not even until this advantage is in some way erased. Another way of putting it is that he owes something to others, for he has something that does not rightfully belong to him. Justice—that is, punishing such individuals—restores the equilibrium of benefits and burdens by taking from the individual what he owes, that is, exacting the debt.[12]

A just legal system creates a mutually beneficial system of cooperation. Because members of society bear the burden of restraining themselves to abide by the law (even when lawbreaking might be tempting or in their interest), a benefit is created for everyone, namely, security of persons and possessions, not to mention regularity and predictability and the like. The lawbreaker is one who takes this benefit but refuses to bear the burden of self-restraint. He thus violates the principle of fairness, of which John Rawls writes, "[t]he main idea is that when a number of persons engage in a mutually advantageous cooperative venture according to rules, and thus restrict their liberty in ways necessary to yield advantages for all, those who have submitted to these restrictions have a right to a similar acquiescence on the part of those who have benefited from their submission."[13]

---

11. Ibid., 37.

12. Herbert Morris, "Persons and Punishment," in *Punishment and the Death Penalty: The Current Debate*, ed. R. M. Baird and S. E. Rosenbaum (Amherst, NY: Prometheus Books, 1995), 63.

13. John Rawls, *A Theory of Justice* (Cambridge, MA: Harvard University Press, 1971), 112; Rawls expresses indebtedness for this statement of the principle to H. L. A. Hart, "Are There Any Natural Rights?" *Philosophical Review* 64 (1955): 185f.

Michael Davis has tried to formulate a version of the fairness justification of punishment; he calls it the *unfair-advantage principle*. Continuing in the same vein as Morris, Davis writes: "Anyone who breaks a law does not bear the same burden the [law-abiding] rest do. Unless he is punished, he will, in effect, have gotten away with doing less than others. He will have an advantage they do not. According to the unfair-advantage principle, it is this advantage that the criminal law is supposed to take back by punishing the criminal for his crime."[14] Note, as it will be important later, that Davis understands this principle as a form of retributivism—an alternative, within retributivism, to the *lex talionis*. Because the unfair-advantage principle and the *lex talionis* measure punishment in different ways—the former by the value of the advantage unfairly taken from the law-abiding and the latter by the gravity of the harm imposed—the two rationales are likely to yield incompatible prescriptions for punishment:

> The advantage [that the criminal law is supposed to take back by punishing the criminal for his crime] bears no necessary relation to the harm the criminal actually did. . . . According to the unfair-advantage principle, the damage a criminal actually does is between him and his victim, a private matter to be settled by civil suit (or the moral equivalent). His *crime* consists only in the unfair advantage he necessarily took over the law-abiding by breaking the law in question. The measure of punishment due is the relative value of *that* advantage. The greater the advantage, the greater the punishment should be. The focus of the unfair-advantage principle is on what the *criminal* gained; the focus of *lex talionis*, on what *others* lost.[15]

Davis goes on to point to cases in which the *lex talionis* cannot, but the unfair-advantage principle can, account for the amount of punishment that appears justified. For example, Davis notes that Illinois, like many American and foreign jurisdictions, distinguishes the crimes of involuntary manslaughter and vehicular homicide, punishing the former with two to five years of imprisonment and the latter with one to three years of imprisonment. Both have the same mental requirement for guilt, recklessness, and the same harm, death. Accordingly, Davis maintains that *lex talionis* cannot account for the distinction between the penalties, nor may we dismiss it as an anomaly in view of how many legal systems recognize a similar distinction. Davis contends that the unfair-advantage principle can ac-

---

14. Michael Davis, "Harm and Retribution," 192.
15. Ibid.

count for the difference. He proposes that, to compare the unfair advantage in the two crimes, we should imagine that licenses to commit the two crimes with impunity were up for auction. Then, since "a license to commit involuntary manslaughter in any way whatever is more useful than a license to commit it in only one way, by use of a vehicle," the unfair advantage taken by the criminal who commits involuntary manslaughter is more valuable than that taken by the one who commits vehicular homicide. And this accounts for the greater punishment attached to involuntary manslaughter.[16]

Likewise, Davis thinks that *lex talionis* cannot explain recidivist statutes—such as the infamous "three strikes and you're out" laws that have recently been passed in a number of states—which impose extremely harsh punishment on people convicted of a third serious crime (punishment that may be more than the sum of the punishments for each of the three crimes). Even if a defender of *lex talionis* were to maintain that a repeat offender shows a deeper and more profound commitment to evil (greater "inner viciousness"), this will surely not account for the enormous difference in punishment for a third offense compared to the punishment that would be meted out for the same crime (and thus for the same harm) by a first offender. Davis contends that, by contrast, no such problem faces the unfair-advantage principle. As long as there is a rule against repeat offenses, a repeat offender takes a separate and additional advantage that a first offender does not take, though they commit the same offenses, and thus the recidivist deserves a punishment beyond that deserved by the first offender.[17]

Whether or not one is persuaded by Davis's analyses of these cases, I

---

16. Ibid., 207–12. This explanation of Davis's is not very satisfactory. Imagine two similar states with identical criminal justice systems, except that in one there is a single law against all involuntary manslaughter no matter what the implement used (vehicle, gun, hammer, etc.), and in the other there are separate laws against involuntary manslaughter for each implement with which one might commit that crime. If a person in each society commits involuntary manslaughter with the same implement (in the same way, etc.), the person in the first society will be charged under the general law and the person in the second will be charged under the law that specifies the implement used. According to Davis's suggestion, we would have to say that the person in the first society took greater advantage of the law-abiding than the person in the second society even though both performed the very same antisocial act. This doesn't seem plausible.

17. Ibid., 200.

think they do serve to show that his basic point is correct: There is a divergence between the punishments that *lex talionis* justifies and those justified by the fairness rationale. The former measures punishment by the harm imposed on the victim, while the latter measures punishment by the advantage taken by the criminal—and there is no reason to think these will coincide: "The advantage bears no necessary relation to the harm the criminal actually did."[18] In fact, there is considerable reason to think they will diverge, as Davis's examples suggest.

Since punishments based on the fairness rationale are likely to diverge from those justified by *lex talionis*, the former may turn out to be more or less than the latter. But then, recalling Goldman's argument, punishments based on fairness will either be more than *lex talionis* allows (and thus unjust according to traditional retributivism, for which *lex talionis* is the upper limit of just punishment) or less than deterrence needs. Consequently, there is no way to combine these different rationales for punishment into a single internally consistent standard. Or so it seems.

2. Combining the Three Rationales into One Measure of Justly Deserved Punishment

I want to suggest that this problem can be overcome. All of the rationales for punishment can be seen as forms of just desert, and thus they can be combined into a single internally consistent standard for determining how much punishment is justified. To show this, let me start by assuming a point that I will actually defend in the following section, namely, that the traditional (*lex talionis*) retributivist justification is already a theory of just desert: A criminal justly deserves the equivalent to the harm he has intentionally imposed on his victim. Let us look, then, at the other two rationales: fairness and deterrence.

We noted earlier that Davis takes the fairness rationale to be a form of retributivist justification of punishment. I don't think this is quite correct. Insofar as Davis holds that punishment is meant to "take back" the advantage that the criminal unfairly took, this seems more like *restitution* (to society) than *retribution* (to the offender). Normally, we would think that punishment is added on top of taking back the advantage a criminal took. (If you stole $100 from someone, you would certainly owe that money to

---

18. Ibid., 192.

your victim, and it would certainly be right to make you pay it back. And *then* you would be punished.) The point here is that taking back the advantage that the criminal took restores things to the way they were before the crime. And that is restitution, not retribution: Restitution involves restoring the *status quo ante,* the condition prior to the offense. However, since it was in this condition that the criminal's offense was committed, this condition constitutes the baseline from which retribution is exacted. Thus retribution involves imposing a loss on the offender measured from the status quo ante. It inherently requires making the criminal worse off than he was before the crime, and thus must do more than take back the criminal's unfairly taken advantage. Returning a thief's loot to his victim so that thief and victim now own what they did before the offense is restitution. Taking enough from the thief so that what he is left with is less than what he had before the offense is retribution, since that is just what the thief did to his victim, namely, make him worse off than he was before the offense.

Put otherwise, taking back the unfair advantage rectifies the fact that the criminal *has* an unfair advantage, and thus taking back the advantage would be appropriate even if the criminal had ended up with it without foul play. But that very fact shows that taking back the unfair advantage does nothing about the criminal's crime, which was the *taking* (not just the *having*) of that advantage. Consequently, a retributivist may punish *for* taking unfair advantage, but the punishment must be something other than taking back that advantage.

If the fairness rationale justifies punishment *for* taking unfair advantage, then, rather than pointing to a separate justification for punishment, the fairness view points to a separate harm caused by the offender—other than the harm caused to his immediate victim. This separate harm is a distinctly *social* harm. Unlike the harm of broken bones, this harm is possible only because a rule-governed cooperative arrangement exists, and the recipients of this harm are all the people who play by the rules on the expectation that others will play by the rules as well.

If the fairness rationale points to a distinct harm for which offenders are to be punished, we will need a justification for that punishment that fairness itself cannot provide. Fairness may—à la Morris and Davis—require taking back the unfair advantage, but fairness does not require this (or anything else) *as* punishment. The fairness view, then, is not really a justification for punishment at all; it is an elucidation of the nature of criminal harm. Having recognized that the criminal harms society by taking advantage of law-abiders, we will still need to know why it is justified to punish criminals for this after the advantage has been taken back. And to answer this we will have to appeal to one or both of the other two rationales: It is justified to punish criminals for taking unfair advantage (via retributivism) as payback for this particular harm or (via deterrence) to discourage potential criminals from so harming their fellows. (Note that, though these considerations will effectively assimilate the fairness account to that of retribution and deterrence, I shall continue to speak of fairness as a distinct rationale for punishment because it refers to a distinct harm that ought to be punished.) Punishment on the fairness rationale will be the offender's just deserts if, in the following section, I can redeem the assumption made in this section that retributive punishment is justly deserved, and more so if I can show that deterrent punishment is justly deserved, to which I turn now.

It may seem impossible to show that the punishment justified by deterrence is also a matter of just desert. Traditionally, deterrence has been given as a utilitarian rationale for punishment, in which suffering imposed on actual criminals is justified by its tendency to dissuade others from committing crimes, thereby reducing suffering overall. Far from being deserved by the criminal because of the evil she has done, punishment can work as deterrence even if the one punished is innocent and only publicly believed to be guilty. For the utilitarian, the relationship between guilt and punishment is a pragmatic one. We get a deterrent effect only if we punish individuals who are believed to be guilty. If individuals believed innocent were also punished, then citizens would not be able to avoid punishment by avoiding crime, and thus there would be no incentive to do so. As a practical matter, the safest way to punish people who are believed guilty is to punish those who are guilty. But then they are not punished because they deserve it; they are punished because, as a matter of practical fact, doing so is the best way to get other people to refrain from committing crimes.

However, the deterrence justification of punishment need not be based on utilitarianism. It can be arrived at in a different way, namely, as an expression of people's right to self-protection. I say "self-protection" rather than "self-defense" because the latter has a familiar legal meaning that appears to exclude deterrence. Legally, self-defense permits only as much physical resistance (including violence) as is needed to stop an ongoing attack. The idea of stopping attacks by threatening a harm that will be imposed only *after* the attack is over is not thought of as part of self-defense, as this is used in courts of law to justify violent acts that would normally be illegal. Nonetheless, Warren Quinn has made a convincing case that threats of post-attack harms are morally indistinguishable from what normally comes under self-defense, and therefore such threats can be thought of as permissible exercises of our right to protect ourselves from unjustified attacks.

Quinn takes it as uncontroversial that, to protect ourselves against unjustified violations of our rights, "we may arrange that an automatic cost *precede* or *accompany* the violation of some right, a cost not designed to frustrate the violation but rather to provide a strong reason not to attempt it. The one-way tire spikes placed at the exits of private parking areas [to dissuade drivers from entering through the exits] provide a commonplace example."[19] Given that we seem to have a right to protect ourselves in this way, Quinn contends that there is no moral reason that we cannot extend this right into a right to threaten harms that would occur subsequent to violations. He writes,

> Suppose the best fence that someone in the state of nature can erect to block an attack on his life cannot stop some vigorous and agile enemies. He would then, under this right [to protect oneself by arranging harms that accompany violations], be permitted to place dangerous spikes at the top of the fence in order to discourage those who could otherwise scale it. These spikes, like the more familiar ones in parking lots, would . . . provide most would-be offenders with excellent reasons to hold back. But suppose, to take the story one step further, our defender cannot arrange the spikes so that they offer a threat of injury to someone entering his territory but can arrange them so that they clearly offer a threat of injury to an enemy leaving his territory after an attack. And suppose that the latter arrangement would discourage attacks just as effectively as the former. It would, I submit, be very odd to think that he could have the right to build the first kind of fence but not the second.[20]

I think that Quinn is correct here. The narrow legal definition of "self-defense" is premised on the existence of a functioning legal system that will punish offenders and that aims thereby to replace socially dangerous

---

19. Warren Quinn, "The Right to Threaten and the Right to Punish," in *Punishment*, ed. Simmons et al., 61.
20. Ibid., 63.

retaliation by citizens. Quinn ultimately wants to determine what such a legal system may rightly do, and for that he wants to identify our full right to self-protection by looking at what it seems we may rightly do in the absence of a functioning legal system. This is why he imagines his fence-builder in a state of nature. The right to self-protection we identify there will form the basis for what the legal system may rightly do once it exists. Consequently, we should not imagine ourselves having from the outset only the limited right to self-defense as defined in law. And then it seems that we have the right to protect ourselves by making it costly to attack us, and, if we have that right, it would "be very odd" (as Quinn says) to think we don't have the right to protect ourselves by threatening costs that will be imposed after an attack is completed. Quinn asks,

> What morally relevant difference could it make to a would-be wrongdoer that the injury whose prospect is designed to discourage him will come earlier or later? In either case, the injury is not there to stop him if he tries to attack but rather to motivate him not to attack. But building the second kind of fence is nothing more than creating an automatic cost to *follow* an offense.[21]

But this means that our right to self-protection includes the right to threaten harm that will occur after an attack as a means to motivate a would-be attacker to refrain. And then, when a just state exists with a valid claim to replace private self-protection with public protective mechanisms, the state will also have the right, as its citizens' agent, to threaten harm after offenses as a means to deter criminals from committing them.

What I want to add to this is the following. If we have the right to threaten harms that will follow offenses, and if we do so publicly so that all would-be offenders know it, then we can say that a person who freely chooses to offend voluntarily brings those harms upon himself. And what a person voluntarily brings upon himself that others have a right to impose, he deserves. Note that I am not saying that because a punishment is announced and known in advance therefore an offender deserves the punishment. Rather, my point is that, if we are morally entitled to threaten and eventually to impose a given punishment, then an offender who knowingly does the act for which the punishment is threatened deserves to suffer that punishment. Such an offender chooses to make himself precisely the sort of risk that justifies the threat of punishment originally and

---

21. Ibid.

that suffices to make him deserve punishment when it falls upon him.[22] If this isn't obvious, recall Quinn's strategy of starting from the right to self-defense narrowly construed and expanding that to the self-protective right to threaten punishment. If someone unjustly attacks another person and gets hurt when that person fights back in self-defense, we would normally say that the attacker deserved what he got. But then the person who gets his tires slashed trying to sneak into a parking lot (knowing that the spikes are there) deserves what he gets. So, too, the person who tries to scale the fence with spikes on it. And then, the person who attacks knowing that a legitimately threatened harm will befall him afterward deserves that as well.

How much deterrent punishment is thereby deserved? I think that the answer is that amount needed to deter rational people generally from committing the crime in question. Punishment justified by deterrence must be limited to what will deter *rational people generally* since the law is addressed to rational people generally and, since punishment aimed at deterrence must be threatened in advance, penalties cannot be tailored to different individuals' susceptibilities. Moreover, establishing punishments significantly more severe than are needed to deter rational people generally will surely threaten, and eventually punish, some criminals more than they deserve, and it may end up making the criminal justice system a greater danger to the society than are the criminals it aims to control. Consequently, this view does not allow for extreme punishments simply because they may be needed to deter people who face unusual temptations or who are unusually susceptible to those temptations. It allows, rather, punishment that makes crime generally, to use John Locke's words, "an ill bargain to the offender."[23]

Be clear on what I am not saying. I am not saying that, by committing a crime with a known penalty, a criminal deserves to be used as an example

---

22. None of this should be taken to suggest that we have the right to use force or violence only to protect ourselves against those who choose to endanger us. Far from it. We also have the right to protect ourselves against those who endanger us inadvertently (the accident-prone), or because they could not control themselves (dangerous maniacs). In these cases, however, we would not say that the recipients of our self-protective force or violence *deserved* that force or violence, nor that they were being *punished*.

23. John Locke, *Second Treatise of Government* (Indianapolis, IN: Hackett Publishing, 1980; originally published 1690), 12.

to deter others. Following Quinn, deterrence is justified because our right to self-protection entitles us to make credible threats of punishment before any offense takes place. The carrying out of threatened punishment is simply part of making the threats credible. When she chooses to offend, the offender brings upon herself, and thus deserves, the carrying out of the threat. Unlike retributive punishment, which is justified because the criminal deserves it, deterrent punishment is deserved because it is justified to threaten it.

So far, then, I have assumed (until the next section, when it will be argued) that retributive punishment is deserved, I have argued that deterrent punishment is deserved, and I have argued that punishment for taking unfair advantage is justified by retribution or deterrence or both, and thus it, too, is deserved. If I am correct here, it follows that offenders deserve suffering equivalent to the harms they have intentionally caused, they deserve to be punished for unfairly taking advantage by breaking the rules, and they deserve the protective measures that were rightly threatened as a means to deter them from committing their crimes. Most important, since all are cases of desert, they are all compatible.

What we need, however, is a way of combining the three rationales into a single measure of punishment. Should we, for example, determine the amount of punishment needed to satisfy each rationale and then simply add them up and impose the total amount on the offender?

Not quite, but this proposal suggests a possibility not considered by Davis. He assumes that, if there is a gap between *lex talionis* and some acceptable punishments that can be justified by the unfair-advantage principle, then *lex talionis* must be replaced by the fairness account. He doesn't consider the possibility that that gap might better be narrowed by supplementing *lex talionis* with fairness. Since the taking of unfair advantage *and* the harming of a victim are parts of the wrong done by the criminal, the natural conclusion is that the two are separate grounds of the criminal's rightful punishment. When Davis says that "the damage a criminal actually does is between him and his victim, a private matter to be settled by civil suit (or the moral equivalent). His *crime* consists only in the unfair advantage he necessarily took over the law-abiding by breaking the law," he reveals the flaw in his theory. Would we not have the right to punish people who harm us in a state of nature, or if we met them on some island where there was no law or none that was a component of a cooperative system to which we and they both belonged?[24] The damage and the unfair taking are both parts of the crime, and thus both are rightly punished.

Lex talionis and fairness respond to different components of a crime that each add to the wrong that was done. *Lex talionis* responds to the harm imposed on the victim of a crime and fairness to the advantage taken by the criminal. Since the harm and the unfair advantage are two separate wrongs, they must be added together to give us the total wrong done by the criminal. Accordingly, punishment à la *lex talionis* must be added to punishment à la fairness to yield the punishment that will retribute the offender for the total wrong she did. Then we can say that a criminal deserves the equivalent of the harm she imposed on her victim *plus* the equivalent of the harm she imposed on society by unfairly taking advantage.

What of deterrence then? The danger that a criminal poses and that justifies our threatening punishment to deter him is just the danger that he will cause harm to his victim and take an unfair advantage from the law-abiding. That danger is, then, not a separate component of the wrong the criminal does. Accordingly, it will not do to add an amount of punishment able to deter a given crime on top of the punishment that already satisfies *lex talionis* and fairness. Rather, if the punishment that satisfies those two rationales will also suffice to deter rational people generally from committing the crime, then that punishment will serve all three rationales and give the offender all that he deserves. However, if it takes more punishment to deter rational individuals generally than the amount needed to satisfy the first two rationales, then the least amount of punishment

---

24. "Imagine that, for whatever reason, your society 'dissolved' into disorder and chaos. Once again in your natural state, unprotected by the rule of law, you witness a man brutally robbing and murdering a defenseless victim. If it were within your power to do so, would you not feel justified in seeing to it that the murderer suffered for his crime? Would there be anything morally objectionable in your inflicting on him some harm, either to save others from his atrocities or . . . simply as a response to *what he did*? Would not anyone in the state of nature have a right to *punish* him for his moral crime?" (A. John Simmons, "Locke and the Right to Punish," in *Punishment*, ed. Simmons et al., 223–24; emphasis in original). If you are inclined to answer these three questions yes, no, yes—as I am—then you disagree with Davis that the punishable part of a crime is only its unfairness to the law-abiding. The harm caused is not merely a damage to be recouped privately. It is also rightly subject to punishment.

needed to deter rational individuals generally will satisfy all three rationales and be what the offender deserves.

To shore up this conclusion, I want to show how it enables us to deal with the problems of *lex talionis* versus deterrence pointed to by Goldman, as well as with the problems of *lex talionis* versus fairness that led Davis to think the latter must replace the former. Regarding Goldman's point, we can say that, if a punishment that will satisfy *lex talionis* is still not enough to deter criminals given the low likelihood of apprehension, then, on my view, the punishment can be increased beyond *lex talionis* to the level needed to deter rational people generally. And, contrary to Goldman, no injustice will thereby be done, because the offender deserves that much punishment.

Davis, we saw, pointed to some features of criminal punishment (lesser punishment for vehicular homicide than for involuntary manslaughter, greater punishment for repeat offenders) that could not be accounted for by *lex talionis*. He took this as a reason for replacing *lex talionis* with fairness. But that creates a problem for Davis, the mirror image of the problem he unearthed regarding *lex talionis*. Much as punishing only according to the harm done to the immediate victim can give counterintuitive results when the unfair advantage is not considered, so, too, punishing according to unfair advantage yields counterintuitive results because the harm caused to the victim is not considered. For example, it would seem that the value of the unfair advantage taken of the law-abiding by one who robs a great deal of money is greater than the value of the unfair advantage taken by a murderer, since the latter gets only the advantage of ridding his world of someone he dislikes while the former will be able to make a new life without the one he dislikes and have money left over for other things. Then the unfair-advantage principle leads to the counterintuitive conclusion that such robbers should be punished more severely (and regarded as more wicked) than murderers.[25]

Davis has responded to this type of objection, over several years, by refining his crime-license auction to get it to track the seriousness of the harms caused by crimes. So he has stipulated that the licenses will always

---

25. The fairness rationale for punishment has "counterintuitive implications regarding amounts of punishment for particular crimes, since crimes against property often bring more benefits to their perpetrators than do more serious crimes against persons" (Goldman, "Paradox of Punishment," 32).

be worth at least what others, fearing a particular crime, would pay those who hold licenses for it not to use their licenses; or that the society will, in light of the undesirability of a particular crime, limit the number of available licenses, thereby driving the price up because of scarcity of supply; or that the value of a crime will be a function of the risk of committing it and thus of the degree to which victims are likely to put up a fight; and other equally ingenious provisions.[26]

The need for all these complicated provisions disappears if we think of punishment as being justified by *lex talionis* and fairness and deterrence together. First of all, we will not have to make the advantage taken by the criminal track the seriousness of the harm he caused, because the *lex talionis* component of his punishment will be proportioned to that harm. With the degree of harm left to the side, we can view the unfairness aspect of a crime as constant across crimes. It is simply the unfairness of taking advantage of others' self-restraint, and this is the same harm—and thus deserves the same punishment—no matter what the particular crime is. Then we can say that criminals deserve punishment equivalent to the harm they caused their immediate victim, plus a small punishment premium for the fact that they caused that harm by breaking a law and thus unfairly taking advantage of the law-abiding. If this is not enough to deter rational people generally from committing this crime in the future, then the punishment could be raised until it is enough for that, without doing any injustice to the criminal.

Consider the resources this provides for dealing with the main problem cases that Davis has identified for *lex talionis*. The greater punishment for involuntary manslaughter than vehicular homicide might be due to the fact that vehicular homicide is a crime that virtually any citizen, no matter how otherwise "normal" and law-abiding, stands a fair chance of committing. As a result, the carelessness involved in it may appear to be within the range of normal inadvertence rather than callous or mean-spirited thoughtlessness, and thus the crime would reflect a less evil intention than other forms of recklessness. Its lesser punishment could be accounted for by the distinction that *lex talionis* makes between crimes that reflect

---

26. For the various provisions of his crime-license auction see Davis, "Harm and Retribution," 217–18; as well as Michael Davis, "How to Make the Punishment Fit the Crime," 744; and Michael Davis, *Justice in the Shadow of Death* (Lanham, MD: Rowman & Littlefield, 1996), 244–47, 262–73.

greater or lesser "inner viciousness." Or, it might be the case that, since vehicular homicide is the result of driving recklessly, and since drivers have independent self-interested reasons to drive carefully, vehicular homicide might be judged more easily deterrable than other forms of involuntary manslaughter. And that, too, could account for the former's lesser punishment. Similar resources are available to account for the greater penalties handed out to repeat offenders. Special measures may be needed to deter hardened and experienced criminals, and that, combined with the idea that repeat offenders show a greater "inner viciousness" (their repeated offending being a sign of their profound and abiding commitment to antisocial activities), will justify attaching a recidivist premium to third offenders.

I conclude this section, then, by saying that offenders deserve the least amount of punishment that imposes on them harm equivalent to the harm they caused their victims *and* the harm they caused to society by taking unfair advantage of the law-abiding *and* that will effectively deter rational people generally from committing such crimes in the future.

II. Death and Desert

In this section, I aim to show that execution is justly deserved punishment for some murders, *as a step toward arguing that it is not unjust to punish murder less harshly*. Note, then, that the fact that a punishment is justly deserved does not, in my view, entail that someone has a duty to impose that punishment. Rather, I shall argue in this section that desert creates *a right to punish,* not a duty to do so. To prepare the ground for this argument, I present here three commonplace observations that support the view that desert does not entail a duty to give what is deserved: First, the victim of an offense has the moral right to forgive the offending party rather than punish him though he deserves to be punished; second, we have no duty (not even a prima facie duty) to torture torturers even if they deserve to be tortured; and third, though great benefactors of humanity deserve to be rewarded, no one necessarily has a duty to provide that reward. At most, there is a very weak and easily overridden duty to provide the reward. On the other hand, I will claim that, when the state punishes a criminal, the state has a duty to punish in a way that does not trivialize the harm suffered by the criminal's victim. However, we shall see that this duty is compatible with administering punishment that is less that the full amount deserved.

In my view, the death penalty is a just punishment for murder because the *lex talionis* is just, although, it can be rightly applied only when its implied preconditions are satisfied. In section V, "Just in Principle, Unjust in Practice," I shall spell out those preconditions and argue that the current administration of the death penalty in America fails to satisfy them and is likely to continue so to fail for the foreseeable future.

1. Retributivism, *Lex Talionis,* and Just Desert

There is nothing self-evident about the justice of the *lex talionis* or, for that matter, of retributivism.[27] The standard problem confronting those who would justify retributivism is that of overcoming the suspicion that it does no more than sanctify the victim's desire to hurt the offender back. Since serving that desire amounts to hurting the offender simply for the satisfaction that the victim derives from seeing the offender suffer, and since deriving satisfaction from the suffering of others seems primitive, the policy of imposing suffering on the offender for no other purpose than giving satisfaction to his victim seems primitive as well. Consequently, defending retributivism requires showing that the suffering imposed on the wrongdoer has some worthy point beyond the satisfaction of victims. In what follows, I shall try to identify a proposition—which I call the *retributivist principle*—that I take to be the nerve of retributivism. I think this principle accounts for the justice of the *lex talionis* and indicates the point of the suffering demanded by retributivism. Not to do too much of the work of the death penalty advocate, I shall make no extended argument for this principle beyond suggesting the considerations that make it plausible. I shall identify these considerations by drawing, with some license, on G. W. F. Hegel and Kant.

I think that we can see the justice of the *lex talionis* by focusing on the striking affinity between it and the Golden Rule. The Golden Rule mandates, "Do unto others as you would have others do unto you," while the

---

27. "[T]o say 'it is fitting' or 'justice demands' that the guilty should suffer is only to affirm that punishment is right, not to give grounds for thinking so" (Stanley I. Benn, "Punishment," *The Encyclopedia of Philosophy*, ed. Paul Edwards [New York: Macmillan, 1967], vol. 7, p. 30).

lex talionis counsels, "Do unto others as they have done unto you." It would not be too far-fetched to say that the *lex talionis* is the law enforcement arm of the Golden Rule, at least in the sense that if people were actually treated as they treated others, then everyone would necessarily follow the Golden Rule, because then people could only willingly act toward others as they were willing to have others act toward them. This is not to suggest that the *lex talionis* follows from the Golden Rule, but rather that the two share a common moral inspiration: the equality of persons. Treating others as you *would* have them treat you means treating others as equal to you, because it implies that you count their suffering to be as great a calamity as your own suffering, that you count your right to impose suffering on them as no greater than their right to impose suffering on you, and so on. The notion of the equality of persons leads to the *lex talionis* by two approaches that start from different points and converge.

I call the first approach "Hegelian" because Hegel held (roughly) that crime upsets the equality among persons and that retributive punishment restores that equality by "annulling" the crime.[28] As we have seen, acting according to the Golden Rule implies treating others as your equals. Conversely, violating the Golden Rule implies the reverse: Doing to another what you would *not* have that other do to you violates the equality of persons by asserting a right toward the other that the other does not possess toward you. Doing back to you what you did "annuls" your violation by reasserting that the other has the same right toward you that you assert toward him. Punishment according to the *lex talionis* cannot heal the in-

---

28. "The sole positive existence which the injury [i.e., the crime] possesses is that it is the particular will of the criminal [i.e., it is the criminal's intention that distinguishes criminal injury from, say, injury due to an accident]. Hence to injure (or penalize) this particular will as a will determinately existent is to annul the crime, which otherwise would have been held valid, and to restore the right" (G. W. F. Hegel, *The Philosophy of Right*, trans. T. M. Knox [Oxford: Clarendon Press, 1962; originally published 1821], 69, see also 331n). I take this to mean that the right is a certain equality of sovereignty among the wills of individuals, that crime disrupts that equality by placing one will above others, and that punishment restores the equality by annulling the illegitimate ascendance. On these grounds, as I shall suggest below, the desire for revenge (strictly limited to the desire "to even the score") is more respectable than philosophers have generally allowed. And so Hegel wrote: "The annulling of crime in this sphere where right is immediate [i.e., the condition prior to conscious morality] is principally revenge, which is just in its content in so far as it is retributive" (ibid., 73).

jury that the other has suffered at your hands; rather, it rectifies the indignity he has suffered, by restoring him to equality with you.

This Hegelian account of retributivism provides us with a nonutilitarian conception of crime and punishment. This is so because "equality of persons" here does not mean equality of concern for their happiness, as it might for a utilitarian. On a utilitarian understanding of equality, imposing suffering on a wrongdoer equivalent to the suffering she has imposed would have little point (unless such suffering were exactly what was needed to deter future would-be offenders). Rather, equality of concern for people's happiness would lead us to impose as little suffering on the wrongdoer as is compatible with promoting the happiness of others. Instead of seeing morality as administering doses of happiness to individual recipients, the Hegelian retributivist envisions morality as maintaining the relations appropriate to equally sovereign individuals.[29] A crime, rather than representing a unit of suffering added to the already considerable suffering in the world, is an assault on the sovereignty of an individual that temporarily places one person (the criminal) in a position of illegitimate sovereignty over another (the victim). The victim (or his representative, the state) then has the right to rectify this loss of standing relative to the criminal by meting out a punishment that reduces the criminal's sovereignty to the degree to which she vaunted it above her victim's. It might be thought that this is a duty, not just a right, but that is surely too much. The victim has the right to forgive the violator without imposing punishment. This suggests that it is by virtue of having the right to punish the violator—having authority over the violator's fate equivalent to the authority over the victim's fate that the violator wrongly took—rather than having the duty to punish the violator, that the victim's equality with the violator is restored.

I call the second approach "Kantian" because Kant held (roughly) that, since reason (like justice) is no respecter of the sheer difference among individuals, when a rational being decides to act in a certain way toward his fellows, he implicitly authorizes similar action by his fellows toward

---

29. For this reason, I think this account of crime and punishment is especially appropriate to a liberal moral theory, and I have defended it as such. See my *Justice and Modern Moral Philosophy* (New Haven, CT: Yale University Press, 1990), 187–99, 306–07; and my *Critical Moral Liberalism: Theory and Practice* (Lanham, MD: Rowman & Littlefield, 1997), 235–70, esp. 240.

him.[30] A version of the Golden Rule, then, is a requirement of reason: Acting rationally, one always acts as he would have others act toward him.[31] Consequently, to act toward a person as he has acted toward others is to treat him as a rational being, that is, as if his act were the product of

---

30. According to Kant, "any undeserved evil that you inflict on someone else among the people is one that you do to yourself. If you vilify him, you vilify yourself; if you steal from him, you steal from yourself; if you kill him, you kill yourself." Since Kant held that "[i]f what happens to someone is also willed by him, it cannot be a punishment," he took pains to distance himself from the view that the offender *wills* his punishment. "The chief error contained in this sophistry," Kant wrote, "consists in the confusion of the criminal's [i.e., the murderer's] own judgment (which one must necessarily attribute to his reason) that he must forfeit his life with a resolution of the will to take his own life" (Kant, "Metaphysical Elements of Justice," 101, 105–106). I have tried to capture this notion of attributing a judgment to the offender, rather than a resolution of his will, with the term "authorizes." This is important, further, because, if we are to stay faithful to Kant, then we must avoid the suggestion that the criminal has willed the universalized version of the maxim on which he acted, since, for Kant, it is precisely the impossibility of willing the universalized version of a maxim that shows the wrongness of acting on that maxim. Thus, for example, R. A. Duff objects to a theory of punishment that might be confused with the theory I develop here, by asking: "How can we say that the criminal has, as a rational being, willed the universalized maxim which justifies his punishment (how can a rational being will what cannot be consistently willed)?" (R. A. Duff, *Trials and Punishments* [New York: Cambridge University Press, 1986], 202). This objection can be sidestepped by insisting that, though the criminal has not willed the universal version of his maxim, he has implicitly affirmed it. This may require moving some distance from Kant, but not a great distance. Kant held that there are two ways in which universalization may fail: some maxims are logically impossible to universalize, and some (though possible to universalize) are impossible to *will* in the universalized form (Immanuel Kant, *Grounding for the Metaphysics of Morals*, trans. J. W. Ellington [Indianapolis, IN: Hackett Publishing, 1981; originally published 1785], 32). If all crimes are of this latter sort, then criminals could be held to affirm their universalization but fail to will it; and, since it is doubtful that Kant ever succeeded in showing that any maxim was logically impossible to universalize, this may be a useful modification of Kant's theory. In any event, since my argument in this essay does not depend on taking a Kantian view of what makes crimes wrong, it is not vulnerable to Duff's criticism.

31. Cf. Kant, *Grounding for the Metaphysics of Morals*, 37n. Kant thinks that the Golden Rule, as commonly stated, places too much emphasis on what an agent *wants*, rather than on what he rationally endorses. Nonetheless, Kant affirms that the Golden Rule is derived from his own central moral principle, the categorical imperative.

a rational decision. From this, it may be concluded that we have a duty to do to offenders what they have done, since this amounts to according them the respect due rational beings. And Kant asserts as much.[32] Here, too, however, the assertion of a duty to punish seems excessive, since, if this duty arose because doing to people what they have done to others is necessary to accord them the respect due rational beings, then we would have a duty to do to all rational persons *everything*—good, bad, or indifferent—that they do to others. The point, rather, is that, by his acts, a rational being *authorizes* others to do the same to him; he doesn't *compel* them to. Here, again, the argument leads to a right, rather than a duty, to exact the *lex talionis*. It should be clear that the Kantian argument, like the Hegelian one, rests on the equality of persons. A rational agent implicitly authorizes having done to him action similar to what he has done to another only if he and the other are similar in the relevant ways.

The Hegelian and Kantian approaches arrive at the same destination from opposite sides. The Hegelian approach starts explicitly from the victim's equality with the criminal and infers from it the victim's right to do to the criminal what the criminal has done to the victim. The Kantian approach starts explicitly from the criminal's rationality and implicitly from his equality with his victim and infers from these the criminal's authorization of the victim's right to do to the criminal what the criminal has done to the victim. Taken together, these approaches support the following proposition: *The equality and rationality of persons imply that an offender deserves, and his victim has the right to impose on him, suffering equal to that which he imposed on the victim.* This is the proposition I call the *retributivist principle*. This principle provides that the *lex talionis* is the criminal's just desert and the victim's—or, as her representative, the state's—right. Remember that this refers both to what the criminal deserves for harming a particular individual and to what he deserves for unfairly taking advantage of all those who have obeyed the law. Moreover, this principle also indicates the point of retributive punishment, namely, to affirm the equality and rationality of persons, victims and offenders alike. And the point of this affirmation is, like any moral affirmation, to make a statement.

---

32. "Even if a civil society were to dissolve itself by common agreement of all its members . . . , the last murderer remaining in prison must first be executed, so that everyone will duly receive what his actions are worth" (Kant, "Metaphysical Elements of Justice," 102).

It impresses upon the criminal his equality with his victim (which earns him a like fate) and his rationality (by which his actions are held to authorize his fate), and it makes a statement to the society, so that recognition of the equality and rationality of persons becomes a visible part of our shared moral environment that none can ignore in justifying their actions to one another.

I do not contend that it is easy or even always possible to figure out what penalties are equivalent to the harms imposed by offenders. Hugo Bedau, for example, has observed that, apart from murder and possibly some other crimes against the person, "we have no clear intuitions at all about what such equivalences consist in."[33] Even if this is so, however, it is still worth knowing what the criterion of deserved punishment is. At very least, it gives us a way of critiquing penalties that strike us as way out of line with the crimes they retribute. Moreover, if there are some crimes—murder and other crimes against the person—for which we do have clear intuitions about the equivalences, we might be able to fill in much of the rest of a scheme of retributive penalties by using our less-than-clear intuitions about other crimes to make ordinal judgments of relative severity. In any event, knowing what criminals deserve according to *lex talionis* gives us something at which to aim, a target in light of which we might eventually sharpen our intuitions.

When I say that, with respect to the criminal, the point of retributive punishment is to impress upon him his equality with his victim, I mean to be understood quite literally. If the sentence is just and the criminal rational, then the punishment should normally *force* upon him recognition of his equality with his victim, recognition of their shared vulnerability to suffering and their shared desire to avoid it, as well as recognition of the fact that he counts for no more than his victim in the eyes of their fellows. For this reason, the retributivist requires that the offender be sane not only at the moment of his crime, but also at the moment of his punishment— while this latter requirement would be largely pointless (if not downright malevolent) to a utilitarian. Incidentally, it is, I believe, the desire that the offender be forced by suffering punishment to recognize his equality with his victim, rather than the desire for that suffering itself, that constitutes what is rational in the desire for revenge.[34]

---

33. Hugo Bedau, personal correspondence to author.
34. See note 28 above.

The retributivist principle represents a conception of moral desert the complete elaboration of which would take us beyond the scope of the present essay. In its defense, however, it is worth noting that our common notion of moral desert includes (at least) two elements: (1) a conception of individual responsibility for actions that is "contagious," that is, one that confers moral justification on the punishing (or rewarding) reactions of others; and (2) a measure of the relevant cost of actions that determines the legitimate magnitude of justified reactions. Broadly speaking, the Kantian notion of authorization implicit in rational action supplies the first element, and the Hegelian notion of upsetting and restoring equality of persons supplies the second. It seems, then, reasonable to take the equality and rationality of persons as implying moral desert in the way asserted in the retributivist principle. I shall assume henceforth that the retributivist principle is true.

2. The Top and the Bottom End of the Range of Just Punishments

The truth of the retributivist principle establishes that *lex talionis* is the offender's just desert; but, since it establishes this as a right of the victim rather than the victim's duty, it does not settle the question of whether or to what extent the victim or the state ought to exercise this right and exact the *lex talionis*. This is a separate moral question because strict adherence to the *lex talionis* amounts to allowing criminals, even the most barbaric of them, to dictate our punishing behavior. As Bedau points out, "Where criminals set the limits of just methods of punishment, as they will do if we attempt to give exact and literal implementation to *lex talionis*, society will find itself descending to the cruelties and savagery that criminals employ."[35] It seems certain that there are at least some crimes, such as rape or torture, that we ought not to try to match. And this is not merely a matter of imposing an alternative punishment that produces an equivalent amount of suffering, as, say, some number of years in prison that might "add up" to the harm caused by a rapist or a torturer. Even if no amount of time in prison would add up to the harm caused by a torturer, it still seems that we ought not to torture him even if this were the only way of making him suffer as much as he has made his victim suffer. Or consider someone who has committed several murders in cold blood. On the *lex*

---

35. Bedau, "Capital Punishment," 176.

talionis, it would seem that such a criminal might justly be brought to within an inch of death and then revived (or to within a moment of execution and then reprieved) as many times as he has killed (minus one), and then finally executed. But surely this is a degree of cruelty that would be monstrous.

Since the retributivist principle establishes the *lex talionis* as the victim's right, it might seem that the question of how far this right should be exercised is "up to the victim." Indeed, this would be the case in the state of nature. But once, for all the good reasons familiar to readers of Locke, the state comes into existence, public punishment replaces private, and the victim's right to punish reposes in the state. With this, the decision as to how far to exercise this right goes to the state as well. To be sure, since (at least with respect to retributive punishment) the victim's right is the source of the state's right to punish, the state must exercise its right in ways that are faithful to the victim's right. When I try to spell out the upper and lower limits of just punishment, these limits may be taken as indicating the range within which the state can punish and remain faithful to the victim's right.

I suspect that it will be widely agreed that the state ought not to administer punishments of the sort described above even if required by the letter of the *lex talionis* and that, thus, even granting the justice of *lex talionis*, there are occasions on which it is morally appropriate to diverge from its requirements. We must distinguish such morally based divergence from divergence based on practicality. Like any moral principle, the *lex talionis* is subject to "ought implies can," that morality cannot ask more of us than is practically possible. It will usually be impossible to do to an offender exactly what she has done—for example, her offense will normally have had an element of surprise that is not possible for a judicially imposed punishment—but this fact can hardly free her from having to bear the suffering she has imposed on another. Thus, for reasons of practicality, the *lex talionis* must necessarily be qualified to call for doing to the offender *as nearly as possible* what she has done to her victim. When, however, we refrain from raping rapists or torturing torturers, we do so for reasons of morality, not of practicality. And, given the justice of the *lex talionis*, these moral reasons cannot amount to claiming that it would be unjust to rape rapists or torture torturers. Rather, the claim must be that, even though it would be just to rape rapists and torture torturers, other moral considerations weigh against doing so.

On the other hand, when, for moral reasons, we refrain from exacting the *lex talionis* and impose a less harsh alterative punishment, it cannot automatically be the case that we are doing an injustice to the victim. Otherwise, we would have to say it was unjust to imprison our torturer rather than torturing him or to simply execute our multiple murderer rather than "multiply executing" him. Surely it is counterintuitive (and irrational to boot) to set the demands of justice so high that a society would have to choose between being barbaric and being unjust. That would effectively price justice out of the moral market.

The implication of the notion that justice permits us to avoid extremely cruel punishments is that there is a range of just punishments that includes some that are just though they exact less than the full measure of the *lex talionis*. What are the top and bottom ends of this range? In considering this question, remember that I argued that punishment sufficient to deter rational people generally is part of what a criminal deserves, and that punishment insufficient to deter does injustice to potential criminals. It follows that all punishments within the range of just punishments must be sufficient to deter rational people generally from the crime in question. Assume, then, for purposes of simplicity, that we are trying to identify the range of just punishments from within a series of punishments of increasing harshness all of which suffice to provide adequate deterrence.

Within this series of punishments, the top end of the range of just punishments is given by *lex talionis*, and the bottom end is, in a way, as well. Based on the argument of the previous section, the top end, the point after which more or harsher punishment is undeserved and thus unjust, is reached when we impose a punishment that is equivalent to the harm caused by the criminal (including both the harm done to his immediate victim and the harm done to the law-abiding by his unfair taking of advantage). As for the bottom end, recall that, if the retributivist principle is true, then denying that the offender deserves suffering equal to that which she imposed amounts to denying the equality and rationality of persons. From this, it follows that we fall below the bottom end of the range of just punishments when we act in ways that are incompatible with the *lex talionis* at the top end. We do injustice to the victim when we treat the offender in a way that is no longer compatible with sincerely believing that she deserves to have done to her what she has done to her victim. In this way, the range of just punishments remains faithful to the victim's right.

This way of understanding just punishment enables us to formulate proportional retributivism so that it is compatible with acknowledging the justice of the *lex talionis*. If we take the *lex talionis* to spell out the offender's just desert, and if other moral considerations require us to refrain from matching the injury caused by the offender while still allowing us to punish justly, then surely we impose just punishment if we impose the closest morally acceptable approximation to the *lex talionis*. Proportional retributivism, then, in requiring that the worst crime be punished by the society's worst punishment and so on, could be understood as translating the offender's just desert into its nearest equivalent in the society's table of morally acceptable punishments. Then, the two versions of retributivism *(lex talionis* and proportional) are related in that the first states what just punishment would be if nothing but the offender's just desert mattered and the second locates just punishment at the meeting point of the offender's just desert and the society's moral scruples.

Inasmuch as proportional retributivism modifies the requirements of the *lex talionis* only in light of other moral considerations, it is compatible with believing that the *lex talionis* spells out the offender's just desert, much in the way that modifying the obligations of promisers in light of other moral considerations is compatible with believing in the binding nature of promises. That a person is justified in failing to keep a promised appointment because she acted to save a life is compatible with still believing that promises are binding. So, too, justifiably doing less than *lex talionis* requires in order to avoid cruelty is compatible with believing that offenders still deserve what *lex talionis* would impose.

Proportional retributivism so formulated preserves the point of retributivism and remains faithful to the victim's right that is its source. Since it punishes with the closest morally acceptable approximation to the *lex talionis*, it effectively says to the offender: You deserve the equivalent of what you did to your victim, and you are getting less only to the degree that our moral scruples limit us from duplicating what you have done. Such punishment, then, affirms the equality of persons by respecting, *as far as seems morally permissible*, the victim's right to impose suffering on the offender equal to what she received, and it affirms the rationality of the offender by treating him as authorizing others to do to him what he has done, though they take him up on it only *as far as it seems to them morally permissible*. Needless to say, the alternative punishments must in some convincing way be comparable in gravity to the crimes that they punish, or else they will trivialize the harms those crimes caused and be no longer compatible with sincerely believing that the offender deserves to have done to him what he has done to his victim and no longer capable of impressing upon the criminal his equality with the victim. If we punish rapists with a small fine, for instance, we do an injustice to their victims because this trivializes the suffering rapists have caused and thus is incompatible with believing that they deserve to have done to them something comparable to what they have done to their victims. If, on the other hand, instead of raping rapists, we impose on them some serious penalty—say, a substantial term of imprisonment—then we do no injustice even though we refrain from exacting the *lex talionis*.[36]

To sum up: When, because we are simply unable to duplicate the criminal's offense, we modify the *lex talionis* to call for imposing on the offender as nearly as possible what he has done, we are still at the top end of punishment justified via *lex talionis*, modifying the *lex talionis* only for reasons of practical possibility. When, because of our own moral scruples, we do less than this, we still act justly as long as we punish in a way that is compatible with sincerely believing that the offender deserves the full measure of the *lex talionis*. If this is true, then it is not unjust to spare murderers as long as they can be punished in some other suitably grave way. For example, a natural life sentence with no chance of parole might be a civilized equivalent of the death penalty—after all, people sentenced to life imprisonment have traditionally been regarded as "civilly dead."[37]

It might be objected that no punishment short of death will serve the point of retributivism with respect to murderers because no punishment short of death is commensurate with the crime of murder. For, while some number of years of imprisonment may add up to the amount of harm done by rapists or assaulters or torturers, no number of years will add up to the harm done to the victim of murder. But justified divergence from the *lex*

---

36. For a very thoughtful and provocative discussion of the punishment deserved for rape, see Davis, *Justice in the Shadow of Death*, 183–229.

37. I am indebted to my colleague Robert Johnson for this suggestion. Prisoners condemned to spend their entire lives in prison, Johnson writes, "experience a permanent civil death, the death of freedom. The prison is their cemetery, a 6' by 9' cell their tomb. Interred in the name of justice, they are consigned to mark the passage of their lives in the prison's peculiar dead time, which serves no larger human purpose and yields few rewards. In effect, they give their civil lives in return for the natural lives they have taken" (Robert Johnson, *Death Work: A Study of the Modern Execution Process* [Belmont, CA: Wadsworth Publishing, 1990], 158).

talionis is not limited only to changing the form of punishment while maintaining equivalent severity. Otherwise, we would have to torture torturers rather than imprison them, if they tortured more than could be made up for by years in prison (or by the years available to them to spend in prison, which might be few for elderly torturers), and we would have to subject multiple murderers to "multiple executions." If justice allows us to refrain from these penalties, then justice allows punishments that are not equal in suffering to their crimes. It seems to me that if the objector grants this much, then she must show that a punishment less than death is not merely incommensurate to the harm caused by murder, but so far out of proportion to that harm that it trivializes the harm and thus effectively denies the equality and rationality of persons.

Now, I am vulnerable to the claim that a sentence of life in prison that allows parole after six or eight years does indeed trivialize the harm of (premeditated, cold-blooded) murder. But I cannot see how a sentence that would require a murderer to spend his full natural life in prison, or even the lion's share of his adult life (say, the twenty years between age thirty and age fifty), can be regarded as anything less than extremely severe and thus no trivialization of the harm he has caused. At least with respect to life sentences without parole, there appears to be widespread agreement on this. For example, surveys of Americans in recent years have consistently shown a majority approving of the death penalty for murderers. However, where surveys have offered the choice between the death penalty and life in prison without parole, respondents preferred the latter "*if* imprisonment included financial restitution to the families of victims."[38] And when juries have the possibility of sentencing murderers to life imprisonment without parole, the number of people given death sentences declines dramatically.[39]

---

38. Mark Costanzo and Lawrence T. White, "An Overview of the Death Penalty and Capital Trials: History, Current Status, Legal Procedures, and Cost," *Journal of Social Issues* 50, no. 2 (1994): 9–10. Of surveys that show a majority in favor of the death penalty, a 1995 Gallup Poll is typical. Asked: "Are you in favor of the death penalty for persons convicted of murder?," 77 percent of respondents were in favor, 13 percent were opposed, and 10 percent had no opinion (U.S. Department of Justice, Bureau of Justice Statistics, *Sourcebook of Criminal Justice Statistics, 1994,* ed. Kathleen Maguire and Ann L. Pastore [Washington, DC: U.S. Government Printing Office, 1995], 181).

39. "The number of people given the death sentence in Virginia has plummeted since the state began allowing jurors to sentence murderers to life without

I take it, then, that the justice of the *lex talionis* implies that it is just to
execute murderers, but not that it is unjust to spare them as long as they
are systematically punished in some other suitably grave way—and as long
as the deterrence requirement can be satisfied, to which we now turn.

III. Death and Deterrence

I have maintained that any penalty that is insufficient to deter rational
people from committing the crime to which it is attached falls below the
bottom end of the range of just punishment because it is unjust to potential victims. Thus, were the death penalty proven a better deterrent to the
murder of innocent people than life in prison, we might have to grant the
necessity of instituting the death penalty. But it is far from proven that the
death penalty is a superior deterrent to murder than life in prison, or than
even less harsh but still substantial prison sentences, such as twenty years
without parole.

1. Social Science and the Deterrent Effect of the Death Penalty

Prior to the 1970s, the most important work on the comparative deterrent impact of the death penalty versus life imprisonment was that of
Thorsten Sellin, whose research indicated no increase in the incidence of
homicide in states that abolished the death penalty and no greater incidence of homicide in states without the death penalty compared to similar
states with the death penalty.[40] In 1970, based on a review of the findings
of empirical research on the impact of the death penalty on homicide rates
(including Sellin's study), Hugo Bedau concluded that the claim that the
death penalty is superior to life imprisonment as a deterrent to crimes

---

parole two years ago. . . . Similar declines also have occurred in Georgia and Indi-
ana, two other states that have introduced life without parole in recent years"
(Peter Finn, "Given Choice, Va. Juries Vote for Life," *Washington Post*, February
3, 1997, A1).

40. Thorsten Sellin, *The Death Penalty* (Philadelphia: American Law Institute,
1959). For a summary of pre-1970 deterrence research and additional references,
see William C. Bailey and Ruth D. Peterson, "Murder, Capital Punishment, and
Deterrence: A Review of the Evidence and an Examination of Police Killings,"
Journal of Social Issues 50, no. 2 (1994), esp. 55.

generally, and to the crime of murder particularly, "has been disconfirmed," because the evidence shows uniformly the nonoccurrence of the results that one would expect were the death penalty a superior deterrent.[41] In 1975, Isaac Ehrlich, a University of Chicago econometrician, published the results of a statistical study purporting to prove that, in the period from 1933 to 1969, each execution may have deterred as many as eight murders.[42] This finding was, however, widely challenged.[43] Criticism of Ehrlich's work focuses mainly on the fact that he found a deterrent impact of executions in the period from 1933 to 1969, which includes the period of 1963 to 1969, a time when hardly any executions were carried out and crime rates rose for reasons that are arguably independent of the existence or nonexistence of capital punishment. When the 1963–1969 period is excluded, no significant deterrent effect shows.[44]

In 1978, after Ehrlich's study, the editors of a National Academy of Sciences' study of the impact of punishment wrote: "In summary, the flaws in the earlier analyses (i.e., Sellin's and others) and the sensitivity of the more recent analyses to minor variation in model specification and the serious temporal instability of the results lead the panel to conclude that the available studies provide no useful evidence on the deterrent effect of capital punishment."[45] The authors of a 1996 review of "the vast literature on the question of general deterrence" conclude "that, despite a wide

---

41. Hugo A. Bedau, "Deterrence and the Death Penalty: A Reconsideration," *Journal of Criminal Law, Criminology, and Police Science* 61, no. 4 (1970): 539–48.

42. Isaac Ehrlich, "The Deterrent Effect of Capital Punishment: A Question of Life and Death," *American Economic Review* 65 (June 1975): 397–417.

43. For reactions to Ehrlich's work, see Alfred Blumstein, Jacqueline Cohen, and Daniel Nagin, eds., *Deterrence and Incapacitation: Estimating the Effects of Criminal Sanctions on Crime Rates* (Washington, DC: National Academy of Sciences, 1978), esp. 59–63 and 336–60; Brian E. Forst, "The Deterrent Effect of Capital Punishment: A Cross-State Analysis," *Minnesota Law Review* 61 (May 1977): 743–67; and Deryck Beyleveld, "Ehrlich's Analysis of Deterrence," *British Journal of Criminology* 22 (April 1982): 101–23. For Ehrlich's response to his critics, see Isaac Ehrlich, "On Positive Methodology, Ethics, and Polemics in Deterrence Research," *British Journal of Criminology* 22 (April 1982): 124–39.

44. For a summary of the criticisms of Ehrlich's study, see Victor Kappeler, Merle Blumberg, and Gary Potter, *The Mythology of Crime and Criminal Justice*, 2nd ed. (Prospect Heights, IL: Waveland, 1996), 314–15. See also Bailey and Peterson, "Murder, Capital Punishment, and Deterrence," 55–56.

45. Blumstein et al., eds., *Deterrence and Incapacitation*, 9.

range of methodologies that have been employed to address this issue, there is no evidence that capital punishment is more effective as a deterrent to murder than incarceration."[46]

Note that, while the deterrence research commented upon here generally compares the deterrent impact of capital punishment with that of life imprisonment, the conclusion as to capital punishment's failure to deter murder more than does incarceration goes beyond life in prison. The fact is that, "[i]n the United States, a substantial proportion of inmates serving a life sentence are eventually released on parole."[47] Since this is public knowledge, we should conclude from these studies that capital punishment does not deter murder more effectively than prison sentences that are less than life, though still substantial, such as twenty years.

2. Common Sense and the Deterrent Effect of the Death Penalty

Conceding that it has not been proven that the death penalty deters more murders than life imprisonment, Ernest van den Haag has argued that neither has it been proven that the death penalty does not deter more murders.[48] Thus, his argument goes, we must follow common sense, which teaches that the higher the cost of something, the fewer the people who will choose it. Therefore, at least some potential murderers who would not be deterred by life imprisonment will be deterred by the death penalty. Van den Haag continues:

> [O]ur experience shows that the greater the threatened penalty, the more it deters. . . .
> Life in prison is still life, however unpleasant. In contrast, the death penalty does not just threaten to make life unpleasant—it threatens to take life alto-

---

46. Kappeler et al., *The Mythology of Crime and Criminal Justice*, 325.

47. Ibid., 313.

48. "Other studies published since Ehrlich's contend that his results are due to the techniques and periods he selected, and that different techniques and periods yield different results. Despite a great deal of research on all sides, one cannot say that the statistical evidence is conclusive. Nobody has claimed to have disproved that the death penalty may deter more than life imprisonment. But one cannot claim, either, that it has been proved statistically in a conclusive manner that the death penalty does deter more than alternative penalties. This lack of proof does not amount to disproof" (Ernest van den Haag and John P. Conrad, *The Death Penalty: A Debate* [New York: Plenum, 1983], 65).

gether. This difference is perceived by those affected. We find that when they have the choice between life in prison and execution, 99% of all prisoners under sentence of death prefer life in prison. . . .

From this unquestioned fact a reasonable conclusion can be drawn in favor of the superior deterrent effect of the death penalty. Those who have the choice in practice . . . fear death more than they fear life in prison. . . . If they do, it follows that the threat of the death penalty, all other things equal, is likely to deter more than the threat of life in prison. One is most deterred by what one fears most. From which it follows that whatever statistics fail, or do not fail, to show, the death penalty is likely to be more deterrent than any other.[49]

Those of us who recognize how commonsensical it was, and still is, to believe that the sun moves around the earth will be less willing than van

---

49. Van den Haag and Conrad, *The Death Penalty*, 68–69. An alterative formulation of this "commonsense argument" is put forth and defended by Michael Davis in "Death, Deterrence, and the Method of Common Sense," *Social Theory and Practice* 7, no. 2 (Summer 1981): 145–77. Davis's argument is like van den Haag's except that, where van den Haag claims that people *do* fear the death penalty more than lesser penalties and *are* deterred by what they fear most, Davis claims that it is *rational* to fear the death penalty more than lesser penalties and thus *rational* to be more deterred by it. Thus, he concludes that the death penalty is the most effective deterrent *for rational people*. He admits that this argument is "about rational agents, not actual people" ("Death, Deterrence, and the Method of Common Sense," 157). To bring it back to the actual criminal justice system that deals with actual people, Davis claims that the criminal law makes no sense unless we suppose the potential criminal to be (more or less) "rational" (ibid., 153). In short, the death penalty is the most effective deterrent because it would be rational to be most effectively deterred by it, and we are committed by belief in the criminal law to supposing that people will do what is rational. The problem with this strategy is that a deterrence justification of a punishment is valid only if it proves that the punishment actually deters actual people from committing crimes. If it doesn't prove that, it misses its mark, no matter what we are committed to supposing. Unless Davis's argument is a way of proving that the actual people governed by the criminal law will be more effectively deterred by the death penalty than by lesser penalties, it is irrelevant to the task at hand. And if it is a way of proving that actual people will be better deterred, then it is indistinguishable from van den Haag's version of the argument and vulnerable to the criticisms of it that follow. In his latest version of the commonsense argument, Davis seems to waffle on whether it is about actual people or not. Davis asserts that the commonsense finding that "[t]he death penalty is the most effective deterrent (among those humanely available)" is a *conceptual truth*. And, "[t]he discoveries of social science cannot affect the findings of common sense concerning what would deter

den Haag to follow common sense here, especially when it comes to doing something awful to our fellows. Moreover, there are good reasons for doubting common sense on this matter. Here are three.

1. From the fact that one penalty is more feared than another, it does not follow that the more feared penalty will deter more than the less feared, unless we know that the less feared penalty is not fearful enough to deter everyone who can be deterred—and this is just what we don't know with regard to the death penalty.[50] This point is crucial because it shows that *the commonsense argument includes a premise that cannot be based on common sense,* namely, that the deterrence impact of a penalty rises without limit in proportion to the fearfulness of the penalty. All that common sense could possibly indicate is that deterrence impact increases with fearfulness of penalty *within a certain normally experienced range.* Since few of us ever face a choice between risking death and risking life-time confinement, common sense has no resources for determining whether this difference in fearfulness is still within the range that increases deterrence. To figure that out, we will have to turn to social science—as a matter of common sense! And when we do, we find that most of the research we have on the comparative deterrent impact of execution versus life imprisonment suggests that there is no difference in deterrent impact between the death penalty and life imprisonment.[51]

Since it seems to me that whoever would be deterred by a given likelihood of death would be deterred by an *equal* likelihood of life behind bars, I suspect that the commonsense argument only seems plausible because we evaluate it while unconsciously assuming that potential criminals

---

rational agents." Two chapters later, however, Davis writes: "My argument purports to show that, absent proof (or at least strong evidence) that the deterrent tendency of the death penalty is swamped in some way or other, common sense requires us to suppose some deterrent effect" (*Justice in the Shadow of Death,* 21 and 50).

50. "[G]iven the choice, I would strongly prefer one thousand years in hell to eternity there. Nonetheless, if one thousand years in hell were the penalty for some action, it would be quite sufficient to deter me from performing that action. The additional years would do nothing to discourage me further. Similarly, the prospect of the death penalty, while worse, may not have any greater deterrent effect than does that of life imprisonment" (David A. Conway, "Capital Punishment and Deterrence: Some Considerations in Dialogue Form," *Philosophy and Public Affairs* 3, no. 4 [Summer 1974]: 433).

51. See notes 40 through 46 above and accompanying text.

will face larger likelihoods of death sentences than of life sentences. If the likelihoods were equal, it seems to me that where life imprisonment were improbable enough to make it too distant a possibility to worry much about, a similar low probability of death would have the same effect. After all, we are undeterred by small likelihoods of death every time we walk the streets. And if life imprisonment were sufficiently probable to pose a real deterrent threat, it would pose as much of a deterrent threat as death. And then it seems that any lengthy prison sentence—say, twenty years— dependably imposed and not softened by parole, would do the same.

2. In light of the fact that the number of privately owned guns in America is substantially larger than the number of households in America, as well as the fact that about twelve hundred suspected felons are killed or wounded by the police in the line of duty every year, it must be granted that anyone contemplating committing a crime already faces a substantial risk of ending up dead as a result.[52] It's hard to see why anyone *who is not already deterred by this* would be deterred by the addition of the more distant risk of death after apprehension, conviction, and appeal.

3. Van den Haag has maintained that deterrence works not only by means of cost-benefit calculations made by potential criminals, but also by the lesson about the wrongfulness of murder that is slowly learned in a society that subjects murderers to the ultimate punishment.[53] If, however, I am correct in claiming that the refusal to execute even those who deserve

---

52. The U.S. Bureau of Alcohol, Tobacco, and Firearms estimated the number of privately owned guns in 1990 at 200,000,000. See Albert Reiss and Jeffrey Roth, eds., *Understanding and Preventing Violence* (Washington, DC: National Academy Press, 1993), 256. For a similar estimate, see Gary Kleck, *Point Blank: Guns and Violence in America* (New York: Aldine de Gruyter, 1991), 17. There are approximately 95,000,000 households in the United States. In a 1979 study, Sherman and Langworthy estimated that between 500 and 700 felons were killed annually by the police in the line of duty (Lawrence W. Sherman and Robert H. Langworthy, "Measuring Homicide by Police Officers," *Journal of Criminal Law and Criminology* 70, no. 4 [Winter 1979]: 546–60). Public outcry and better training seem to have lowered this number to around 400. The FBI reports 462 such killings in 1994 and 383 in 1995 (Federal Bureau of Investigation, *Uniform Crime Reports for the United States: 1995* [Washington, D.C.: U.S. Government Printing Office, 1996], 22). A survey of studies of police shootings by Binder and Fridell concludes that "approximately 30 percent of persons shot by the police will actually die" (in Kappeler et al., *The Mythology of Crime and Criminal Justice*, 214).

53. Van den Haag and Conrad, *The Death Penalty*, 63.

it has a civilizing effect, then the refusal to execute also teaches a lesson about the wrongfulness of murder. My claim here is admittedly speculative, but no more so than van den Haag's to the contrary. And my view has the added virtue of accounting for the failure of research to show an increased deterrent effect from executions, *without having to deny the plausibility of van den Haag's commonsense argument that at least some additional potential murderers will be deterred by the prospect of the death penalty.* If there is a deterrent effect from *not executing,* then it is understandable that while executions will deter some murderers, this effect will be balanced out by the weakening of the deterrent effect of not executing, such that no net reduction in murders will result.[54] This, by the way, also disposes of van den Haag's argument that, in the absence of knowledge one way or the other on the deterrent effect of executions, we should execute murderers rather than risk the lives of innocent people whose murders might have been deterred if we had executed. If there is a deterrent effect of not executing, it follows that we risk innocent lives either way. And if this is so, it seems that the only reasonable course of action is to refrain from imposing what we know is a horrible fate.[55]

---

54. A related claim has been made by those who defend the so-called brutalization hypothesis by presenting evidence to show that murders increase following an execution. See, for example, William J. Bowers and Glenn L. Pierce, "Deterrence or Brutalization: What Is the Effect of Executions?" *Crime and Delinquency* 26, no. 4 (October 1980): 453–84. Bowers and Pierce conclude that each execution gives rise to two additional homicides in the month following and that these are real additions, not just a change in timing of the homicides (481). My claim, it should be noted, is not identical to this, since, as I indicate in the text, what I call "the deterrent effect of not executing" is not something whose impact is to be seen immediately following executions, but an effect that occurs over the long haul; further, my claim is compatible with finding no net increase in murders due to executions. Nonetheless, should the brutalization hypothesis be borne out by further studies, it would certainly lend support to the notion that there is a deterrent effect of not executing.

55. Van den Haag writes: "If we were quite ignorant about the marginal deterrent effects of execution, we would have to choose—like it or not—between the certainty of the convicted murderer's death by execution and the likelihood of the survival of future victims of other murderers on the one hand, and on the other his certain survival and the likelihood of the death of new victims. I'd rather execute a man convicted of having murdered others than put the lives of innocents at risk. I find it hard to understand the opposite choice" (van den Haag and Conrad, *The Death Penalty,* 69). Conway was able to counter this argument earlier by pointing

I conclude then that we have no good reason to think that we need the death penalty to protect innocent people from murder. Life in prison (or, at least, a lengthy prison term without parole) dependably meted out, will do as well.

IV. Pain and Civilization

The arguments of the previous two sections prove that, though the death penalty is a just punishment for murder, no injustice is done to actual or potential victims if we refrain from imposing the death penalty. In this section, I shall show that, in addition, there are good moral reasons for refraining.

The argument that I gave for the justice of the death penalty for murderers proves the justice of beating assaulters, raping rapists, and torturing torturers. Nonetheless, I take it that it would not be right for us to beat assaulters, rape rapists, or torture torturers, *even though it were their just deserts*—and even if this were the only way to make them suffer as much as they made their victims suffer. Calling for the abolition of the death penalty, though it be just, then, amounts to urging that we as a society place execution in the same category of sanction as beating, raping, and torturing and treat it as something it would also not be right for us to do to offenders, *even if it were their just deserts*.

To argue for placing execution in this category, I must show what would be gained therefrom. To show that, I shall indicate what we gain from placing torture in this category and argue that a similar gain is to be had from doing the same with execution. I select torture because I think the

---

out that the research on the marginal deterrent effects of execution was *inconclusive*, not in the sense of *tending to point both ways*, but rather in the sense of *giving us no reason to believe that capital punishment saves more lives than life imprisonment*. He could then answer van den Haag by saying that the choice is, not between risking the lives of murderers and risking the lives of innocents, but between killing a murderer with no reason to believe lives will be saved and sparing a murderer with no reason to believe lives will be lost (Conway, "Capital Punishment and Deterrence," 442–43). This, of course, makes the choice to spare the murderer more understandable than van den Haag allows. While the great majority of studies still support Conway's argument here, that claim is weakened by the advent of Ehrlich's research, which, contested though it may be, is research that points the other way.

reasons for placing it in this category are, due to the extremity of torture, most easily seen—but what I say here applies with appropriate modification to other severe physical punishments, such as beating and raping. First, and most evident, placing torture in this category broadcasts the message that we as a society judge torturing so horrible a thing to do to a person that we refuse to do it even when it is deserved. Note that such a judgment does not commit us to an absolute prohibition on torturing. No matter how horrible we judge something to be, we may still be justified in doing it if it is necessary to prevent something even worse. Leaving this aside for the moment, what is gained by broadcasting the public judgment that torture is too horrible to inflict even if deserved?

1. The Advancement of Civilization and the Modern State

I think that the answer to the question just posed lies in what we understand as civilization. In *The Genealogy of Morals,* Friedrich Nietzsche says that in early times "pain did not hurt as much as it does today."[56] The truth in this intriguing remark is that progress in civilization is characterized by a lower tolerance for one's own pain and that suffered by others. And this is appropriate, since, via growth in knowledge, civilization brings increased power to prevent or reduce pain, and, via growth in the ability to communicate and interact with more and more people, civilization extends the circle of people with whom we empathize.[57] If civilization is characterized by lower tolerance for our own pain and that of others, then publicly refusing to do horrible things to our fellows both signals the level of our civilization *and, by our example, continues the work of civilizing.* This gesture is all the more powerful if we refuse to do horrible things to

---

56. Friedrich Nietzsche, *The Genealogy of Morals,* in *The Birth of Tragedy and the Genealogy of Morals,* trans. Francis Golffing (New York: Doubleday, 1956; originally published 1887), 199–200.

57. Van den Haag writes that our ancestors "were not as repulsed by physical pain as we are. The change has to do not with our greater smartness or moral superiority but with a new outlook pioneered by the French and American revolutions [namely, the assertion of human equality and with it 'universal identification'], and by such mundane things as the invention of anesthetics, which make pain much less of an everyday experience" (van den Haag and Conrad, *The Death Penalty,* 215); cf. van den Haag's *Punishing Criminals* (New York: Basic Books, 1975), 196–206.

those who deserve them. I contend, then, that the more horrible things we are able to include in the category of what we will not do, the more civilized we are and the more civilizing. Thus we gain from including torture in this category, and, if execution is especially horrible, we gain still more by including it.

But notice, it is not just any refraining from horrible punishments that is likely to produce this gain. It is important to keep in mind that I am talking about modern states, with their extreme visibility, their moral authority (tattered of late but not destroyed), and their capacity to represent millions, even hundreds of millions, of citizens. It is when modern states refrain from imposing grave harms on those who deserve them that a powerful message about the repugnant nature of such harms is broadcast. It is this message that I contend contributes to civilization by increasing people's repugnance for such harmful acts generally. And, I believe that, because of modern states' unique position—their size, visibility, and moral authority, modern states have a duty to act in ways that advance civilization.

Needless to say, the content, direction, and even the worth of civilization are hotly contested issues, and I shall not be able to win those contests in this brief space. At a minimum, however, I take it that civilization involves the taming of the natural environment and of the human animals in it, and that the overall trend in human history is toward increasing this taming, though the trend is by no means unbroken or without reverses. On these grounds, we can say that growth in civilization generally marks human history, that a reduction in the horrible things we tolerate doing to our fellows (even when they deserve them) is part of this growth, and that, once the work of civilization is taken on consciously, it includes carrying forward and expanding this reduction. It might be objected that this view of civilization is ethnocentric, distinct to citizens of modern Western states but not shared, say, by hardy nomadic tribes. My response is that, while I do not believe the view is limited in this way, if it is, then so be it. I am, after all, addressing the citizens of a modern Western state and urging that they advance civilization by refraining from imposing the death penalty. What other guide should these citizens use than their own understanding of what constitutes civilization?

Some evidence for the larger reach of my claim about civilization and punishment is found in what Émile Durkheim identified, nearly a century ago, as "two laws which seem . . . to prevail in the evolution of the apparatus of punishment." The first, the *law of quantitative change*, Durkheim formulates thusly:

> The intensity of punishment is the greater the more closely societies approximate to a less developed type—and the more the central power assumes an absolute character.

And the second, which Durkheim refers to as the *law of qualitative change*, is this:

> Deprivations of liberty, and of liberty alone, varying in time according to the seriousness of the crime, tend to become more and more the normal means of social control.[58]

Several things should be noted about these laws. First of all, they are not two separate laws. As Durkheim understands them, the second exemplifies the trend toward moderation of punishment referred to in the first.[59] Second, the first law really refers to two distinct trends, which usually coincide but do not always. Moderation of punishment accompanies both the movement from less to more advanced types of society and the movement from more to less absolute rule. Normally these go hand in hand, but where they do not, the effect of one trend may offset the effect of the other. Thus, a primitive society without absolute rule may have milder punishments than an equally primitive, but more absolutist, society.[60] This complication need not trouble us, since the claim I am making refers to the first trend, namely, that punishments tend to become milder as societies become more advanced; and that this is a trend in history is not refuted by the fact that it is accompanied by other trends and even occasionally offset by them. Finally, and most important for our purposes, Durkheim's

---

58. Émile Durkheim, "Two Laws of Penal Evolution," *Economy and Society* 2 (1973): 285, 294. This essay was originally published in French in *Année Sociologique* 4 (1899–1900).

59. Durkheim writes that "of the two laws which we have established, the first contributes to an explanation of the second" (ibid., 299).

60. The "two causes of the evolution of punishment—the nature of the social type and of the governmental organ—must be carefully distinguished" (ibid., 288). Durkheim cites the ancient Hebrews as an example of a society of the less-developed type that had milder punishments than societies of the same social type, due to the relative absence of absolutist government among the Hebrews (ibid., 290).

claim that punishment becomes less intense as societies become more advanced is a generalization that he supports with an impressive array of evidence from historical societies from pre-Christian times to the time in which he wrote—and this supports my claim that reduction in the horrible things we do to our fellows is in fact part of the advance of civilization.[61]

Against this it might be argued that there are many trends in history, some good, some bad, and some mixed, and thus that the mere existence of some historical trend is not a sufficient reason to continue it. Thus, for example, history is marked generally by growth in population, but we are not for that reason called upon to continue the work of civilization by continually increasing our population. What this suggests is that in order to identify something as part of the work of civilizing, we must show not only that it generally advances over the course of history, but that its advance is, on some independent grounds, clearly an advance for the human species—that is, either an unmitigated gain or at least consistently a net gain. And this implies that even trends we might generally regard as advances may in some cases bring losses with them, such that when they did, it would not be appropriate for us to lend our efforts to continuing them. Of such trends, we can say that they are advances in civilization except when their gains are outweighed by the losses they bring—and that we are called upon to further these trends only when their gains are not outweighed in this way. It is clear, in this light, that increasing population is a mixed blessing at best, bringing both gains and losses. Consequently, population increase is not always an advance in civilization that we should further, though at times it may be.

What can be said of reducing the horrible things that we do to our fellows even when deserved? First of all, given our attitude toward suffer-

---

61. Durkheim's own explanation of the progressive moderation of punishments is somewhat unclear. He rejects the notion that it is due to the growth in sympathy for one's fellows, since this, he maintains, would make us more sympathetic with victims and thus harsher in punishments. He argues instead that the trend is due to the shift from understanding crimes as offenses against God (and thus warranting the most terrible of punishments) to understanding them as offenses against men (thus warranting milder punishments). He then seems to come around nearly full circle by maintaining that this shift works to moderate punishments by weakening the religious sentiments that overwhelmed sympathy for the condemned: "The true reason is that the compassion of which the condemned man is the object is no longer overwhelmed by the contrary sentiments which would not let it make itself felt" (ibid., 303).

ing and pain, it seems clearly a gain. Is it, however, an unmitigated gain? Would such a reduction ever amount to a loss? It seems to me that there are two conditions under which it would be a loss, namely, if the reduction made our lives more dangerous, or if not doing what is justly deserved were a loss in itself. As for the former, as I have already indicated, I accept that if some horrible punishment is necessary to deter equally or more horrible acts, then we might have to impose the punishment. (After all, in self-defense, we accept the imposition by the defender of harms equal to those threatened by his attacker.) Thus my claim is that reduction in the horrible things we do to our fellows is an advance in civilization as *long as our lives are not thereby made more dangerous* and that it is only then that we are called upon to extend that reduction as part of the work of civilization. Assuming, then, that we suffer no increased danger by refraining from doing horrible things to our fellows when they justly deserve them, does such refraining to do what is justly deserved amount to a loss?

The answer to this must be that refraining to do what is justly deserved is a loss only where it amounts to doing an injustice. But such refraining to do what is just is not doing what is unjust, unless what we do instead falls below the bottom end of the range of just punishments. Otherwise, it would be unjust to refrain from torturing torturers, raping rapists, or beating assaulters. If there is no injustice in refraining from torturing torturers, then there is no injustice in refraining from doing horrible things to our fellows generally, when they deserve them, as long as what we do instead is compatible with believing that they do nonetheless deserve those horrible things. Thus, if such refraining does not make our lives more dangerous, then it is no loss, and, given our vulnerability to pain, it is a gain. Consequently, reduction in the horrible things we do to our fellows, when those things are not necessary to our protection, is an advance in civilization.

2. The Horribleness of the Death Penalty

To complete the argument, however, I must show that execution is horrible enough to warrant its inclusion alongside torture. Against this it will be said that execution is not especially horrible, since it only hastens a fate that is inevitable for all of us.[62] I think that this view overlooks important

---

62. Van den Haag seems to waffle on the question of the unique awfulness of

differences in the manner in which people reach their inevitable ends. I contend that execution is especially horrible, and it is so in a way similar to (though not identical with) the way in which torture is especially horrible. I believe we view torture as especially awful because of two of its features, which also characterize execution: intense pain and the spectacle of one person being completely subject to the power of another.[63] This latter is separate from the issue of pain, since it is something that offends us about unpainful things, such as slavery (even voluntarily entered) and prostitution (even voluntarily chosen as an occupation).[64] Execution

---

execution. For instance, he takes it not to be revolting in the way that ear cropping is, because "[w]e all must die. But we must not have our ears cropped" (van den Haag and Conrad, *The Death Penalty*, 190). Here, he cites John Stuart Mill's parliamentary defense of the death penalty, in which Mill maintained that execution only *hastens* death. Mill's point was to defend the claim that "[t]here is not . . . any human infliction which makes an impression on the imagination so entirely out of proportion to its real severity as the punishment of death" (John Stuart Mill, "Parliamentary Debate on Capital Punishment within Prisons Bill," in *Philosophical Perspectives on Punishment*, ed. Gertrude Ezorsky [Albany, NY: State University of New York Press, 1972; Mill made the speech in 1868], 273). Van den Haag seems to agree, since he maintains that, since "we cannot imagine our own nonexistence . . . [t]he fear of the death penalty is in part the fear of the unknown. It . . . rests on a confusion" (*The Death Penalty*, 258–59). On the other hand, he writes: "Execution sharpens our separation anxiety because death becomes clearly foreseen. . . . Further, and perhaps most important, when one is executed he does not just die, he is put to death, forcibly expelled from life. He is told that he is too depraved, unworthy of living with other humans" (ibid., 258). I think, incidentally, that it is an overstatement to say that we cannot imagine our own nonexistence. If we can imagine any counterfactual experience (e.g., how we might feel if we didn't know something that we do in fact know), then it doesn't seem impossible that we can imagine what it would "feel like" not to live. I think I can arrive at a pretty good approximation of this by trying to imagine how things "felt" to me in the eighteenth century. The sense of the awful difference between being and not being alive that enters my experience when I do this makes the fear of death— not as a state, but as the absence of life—seem hardly to rest on a confusion.

63. Hugo Bedau has developed this latter consideration at length with respect to the death penalty. See Hugo A. Bedau, "Thinking about the Death Penalty as a Cruel and Unusual Punishment," *U.C. Davis Law Review* 18 (Summer 1985): 917ff. This article is reprinted in Hugo A. Bedau, *Death Is Different: Studies in the Morality, Law, and Politics of Capital Punishment* (Boston: Northeastern University Press, 1987); and Hugo A. Bedau, ed., *The Death Penalty in America: Current Controversies* (New York: Oxford University Press, 1997).

64. I am not here endorsing this view of voluntarily entered slavery or prostitu-

shares this separate feature, since killing a bound and defenseless human being enacts the total subjugation of that person to his fellows.

Execution, even by physically painless means, is characterized not only by the spectacle of subjugation, but also by a special and intense psychological pain that distinguishes it from the loss of life that awaits us all. Interesting in this regard is the fact that, although we are not terribly squeamish about the loss of life itself, allowing it in war, in self-defense, as a necessary cost of progress, and so on, we are, as the extraordinary hesitance of our courts testifies, quite reluctant to execute.[65] I think this is because execution involves the most psychologically painful features of death. We normally regard death from human causes as worse than death from natural causes, since a humanly caused shortening of life lacks the consolation of unavoidability. And we normally regard death whose coming is foreseen by its victim as worse than sudden death because a foreseen death adds to the loss of life the terrible consciousness of that impending loss.[66] As a humanly caused death whose advent is foreseen by its victim, an execution combines the worst of both. Indeed, it was on just such grounds that Albert Camus regarded the death penalty as itself a kind of torture: "As a general rule, a man is undone by waiting for capital punishment well before he dies. Two deaths are inflicted on him, the first being

---

tion. I mean only to suggest that it is the belief that these relations involve the extreme subjugation of one person to the power of another that is at the basis of their offensiveness. What I am saying is quite compatible with finding that this belief is false with respect to voluntarily entered slavery or prostitution.

65. "[F]or whatever reasons . . . , prosecutors seek the death penalty only in a fraction of all the cases where they could. Again, for a variety of reasons—appropriate mitigating evidence, sympathy for the defendant, lingering doubts about the defendant's guilt—juries bring in a death sentence only in a fraction of all cases where a prosecutor seeks it. When one considers these facts in conjunction with the fact that each capital trial begins by eliminating on the voir dire every prospective juror who evidences opposition to the death penalty, the number of death sentences is surprisingly small" (Hugo A. Bedau, "Interpreting the Eighth Amendment: Principled vs. Populist Strategies," *Thomas M. Cooley Law Review* 13 [1996]: 806).

66. This is no doubt partly due to modern skepticism about an afterlife. Earlier peoples regarded a foreseen death as a blessing allowing time to make one's peace with God. Writing of the early Middle Ages, Philippe Ariès says, "In this world that was so familiar with death, sudden death was a vile and ugly death; it was frightening; it seemed a strange and monstrous thing that nobody dared talk about" (Philippe Ariès, *The Hour of Our Death* [New York: Vintage, 1982], 11).

worse than the second, whereas he killed but once. Compared to such torture, the penalty of retaliation seems like a civilized law."[67]

Thus far, by analogy with torture, I have argued that execution should be avoided because of how horrible it is to the one executed. But there are reasons of another sort that follow from the analogy with torture. Torture is to be avoided not only because of what it says about what we are willing to do to our fellows, but also because of what it says about us who are willing to do it. To torture someone is an awful spectacle not only because of the intensity of pain imposed, but also because of what is required to be able to impose such pain on one's fellows. The tortured body cringes, using its full exertion to escape the pain imposed upon it—it literally begs for relief with its muscles as it does with its cries. To torture someone is to demonstrate a capacity to resist this begging, and that, in turn, demonstrates a kind of hard-heartedness that a society ought not to parade.

This is true not only of torture, but of all severe corporal punishment. Indeed, I think this constitutes part of the answer to the puzzling question of why we refrain from punishments like whipping, even when the alternative (some months in jail versus some lashes) seems more costly to the offender. Imprisonment is painful to be sure, but it is a reflective pain, one that comes with comparing what is to what might have been and that can be temporarily ignored by thinking about other things. But physical pain has an urgency that holds body and mind in a fierce grip. Of physical pain, as Orwell's Winston Smith recognized, "you could only wish one thing: that it should stop."[68] By refraining from torture in particular and corporal punishment in general, we both refuse to put a fellow human being in this grip and refuse to show our ability to resist this wish. The death penalty is the last corporal punishment used officially in the Western world. It is corporal not only because it is administered via the body, but also because the pain of foreseen, humanly administered death strikes its victim with the urgency that characterizes intense physical pain, causing even hardened criminals to cry, faint, and lose control of their bodily functions. There is something to be gained by refusing to endorse the hardness of heart necessary to impose such a fate.

---

67. Albert Camus, "Reflections on the Guillotine," in Albert Camus, *Resistance, Rebellion, and Death* (New York: Knopf, 1961), 205.

68. George Orwell, *1984* (New York: New American Library, 1983; originally published 1949), 197.

By placing execution alongside torture in the category of things we will not do to our fellow human beings even when they deserve them, our state broadcasts the message that totally subjugating a person to the power of others and confronting him with the advent of his own humanly administered demise is too horrible to be done by civilized human beings to their fellows even when they have earned it: too horrible to do, and too horrible to be capable of doing. And I contend that the state's broadcasting this message loud and clear would, in the long run, contribute to the general detestation of murder and be, to the extent to which it worked itself into the hearts and minds of the populace, a deterrent. In short, refusing to execute murderers though they deserve it both reflects and continues the taming of the human species that we call civilization—and it should, over time, contribute to reducing the incidence of murder. Thus, I take it that the abolition of the death penalty, though that penalty is a just punishment for murder, is part of the civilizing mission of modern states.

Notice, before moving on, that I have not here argued that the death penalty is *inhumane*.[69] Inhumane punishments are normally thought to be incompatible with respecting the person of the offender and thus forbidden except perhaps under the most extreme circumstances. Speaking of the death penalty, Kant wrote that "the death of the criminal must be kept entirely free of any maltreatment that would make an abomination of the humanity residing in the person suffering it."[70] Torture almost surely and maybe even execution are inhumane, but I have argued only that they are horrible, that is, that they are punishments that cause their recipients extreme pain, physical and/or psychological. I have tried to show the ways in which the death penalty, even imposed without physical pain, is still a horrible punishment in that it causes extreme psychological suffering often to the point of loss of physical control. I then urged that it would be good for the state to avoid doing such things to people, not simply because it is always morally preferable to impose less pain rather than more, but also because the state—by virtue of its size, high visibility, and moral author-

---

69. Michael Davis takes me to be trying to prove that the death penalty is inhumane, and, since I don't try that, he is able, with predictable ease, to prove that I don't succeed. See Davis, "The Death Penalty, Civilization, and Inhumaneness," *Social Theory and Practice* 16 (Summer 1990): 245–59; and Davis, *Justice in the Shadow of Death*, 47–63.

70. Kant, "Metaphysical Elements of Justice," 102.

ity—is able to have impact on citizens beyond the immediate act it authorizes.

In particular, I have suggested that the state, by the vivid example of its unwillingness to execute even those—*especially those*—who deserve it, would contribute to the process of civilizing humankind, which I take in part to include reducing our tolerance for pain imposed on our fellows. I have called this an advance in civilization for two reasons: first, because history shows that the harshness of punishments seems generally to decline over time, and second, because it seems good to reduce our willingness to impose pain on our fellows. The first condition here is empirical, a matter of what history actually records. And while I think that the elimination of ear cropping, branding, drawing and quartering, and boiling in oil, as well as the practice of throwing members of unpopular religions to the lions for public entertainment, all suggest that the taming that I have in mind is the general trend of history, there are exceptions, of course. The Nazis, for example, tortured their enemies with awful ferocity. But most would recognize Nazism as a step backward in civilization. So, my claim is a broad empirical claim, much in the vein of Richard Rorty's recent suggestion that, in the West, there has been a tendency to want to reduce or eliminate cruelty.[71] But it is equally a moral claim. I have argued that even stable historical trends do not count as advances in civilization unless they are also, on independent grounds, good.[72]

In sum, my argument is that, though the death penalty is just punishment for some murders, execution is a horrible thing to do to our fellows, and, if the state can avoid execution without thereby doing injustice to actual or potential victims of murder, then, in addition to whatever is good about causing less pain, the state would also, by its example, contribute to a general reduction in people's tolerance for doing painful things to one another, a reduction that I think is an advance in civilization. And I think that modern states are morally bound to promote the advance of civilization because they are uniquely positioned to do so and because of the

71. Richard Rorty, *Contingency, Irony, and Solidarity* (Cambridge: Cambridge University Press, 1989), 184–85.

72. Michael Davis incorrectly treats my claim about civilization exclusively as an empirical claim about actual historical trends. See Davis, "The Death Penalty, Civilization, and Inhumaneness," 251; and Davis, *Justice in the Shadow of Death*, 53.

goodness that must characterize a trend if it is to count as an advance in civilization.

Recall that I argued, in section I, that offenders deserve the least amount of punishment that imposes on them harm equivalent to the harm they caused their victims *and* the harm they caused to society by taking unfair advantage of the law-abiding *and* that will effectively deter rational people from committing such crimes in the future. If we take these conjuncts separately, it should be clear from the previous section's argument that the deterrence component can be satisfied with life in prison or some lengthy prison term. Since I take the fairness component to be the same in any crime, it will not in itself add more than a small increment to any particular punishment. Consequently, it, too, should be satisfied if we impose a lengthy prison term on murderers. As for the first component, the *lex talionis* indicates that the murderer justly deserves to die, and nothing I have argued alters this conclusion. However, I have also argued that retribution can be satisfied without executing murderers, so long as they are punished in some other suitably severe way. It follows that, though the death penalty is justly deserved punishment for some murderers, all the rationales for punishment will be satisfied if murderers are sentenced to life in prison or at least to a substantial prison term, such as twenty years without parole. I have argued in the present section that refraining from executing murderers will contribute to the advance of civilization and may, in the long run, reduce the incidence of murder. In sum, there are no moral reasons against, and some very good ones for, abolishing the death penalty. All of this has been based on the idea that the death penalty is just punishment for murder in principle. Additional reasons for abolishing the death penalty appear when we look at it in practice.

V. Just in Principle, Unjust in Practice

On February 3, 1997, the "American Bar Association, the nation's largest and most influential organization of lawyers . . . , voted overwhelmingly to seek a halt to the use of the death penalty, asserting that it is administered through 'a haphazard maze of unfair practices.' "[73]

---

73. Saundra Torry, "ABA Endorses Moratorium on Capital Punishment," *Washington Post*, February 4, 1997, A4.

When it is pointed out to van den Haag that the death penalty has been and is still likely to be administered in an unfair and discriminatory fashion, he replies that the question of the justice of the death penalty and the justice of its administration are two separate questions: "Objections to unwarranted discrimination are relevant to the discriminatory distribution of penalties, not to the penalties distributed."[74] Having said this, van den Haag believes that he has disposed of the objection concerning discrimination, since he has shown that discriminatory application, though admittedly wrong, is not something wrong with the death penalty itself. He is correct in believing that these two questions are distinct and that distinguishing them shields the death penalty from the force of the objection. It does so, however, at a considerable price.

Van den Haag is correct that the justice of a penalty and the justice of a penalty's distribution are theoretically separate matters: We can consistently believe that fining double-parkers in a discriminatory fashion is unjust while believing that fines are a just penalty for double-parking. It is possible to admit that the discriminatory application of a penalty is unjust and still maintain that the penalty itself is in principle a just one. Thus van den Haag can agree with his critics that the discriminatory application of the death penalty is unjust, and still maintain that the penalty itself is in principle a just response to murder. But this way of disposing of the objection carries a high price tag because the very separation of the questions by means of which van den Haag evades the objection dramatically limits the scope of the conclusions he can reach from that point on. Moral assessment of the way a penalty is actually going to be carried out is a necessary ingredient in any determination of the justice of adopting that penalty as our policy. By separating the question of the justice of the death penalty itself from that of the justice of the way it is likely to be carried out, van den Haag separates as well his answer to the question of the justice of the death penalty itself from any answer to the question whether the death penalty is just as an actual policy. As a result, van den Haag may prove that the death penalty is in principle a just response to murder—but at the cost of losing the right to assert that it is just for us to adopt it in practice here and now in America.

If there is reason to believe that a policy will be administered unjustly, then that is reason for believing that it is *unjust* to adopt that policy here

---

74. Van den Haag, *Punishing Criminals*, 221.

and now in America, even though the policy is just in principle. This is not to say that injustice in the administration of a policy automatically makes it wrong to adopt the policy. It might still be that all the available alternatives are worse, such that, on balance, we do better by adopting this policy than by adopting any of the other possible candidates. However, in the absence of a showing that all alternatives are worse, I take it that it is wrong to adopt an unjust policy, and thus that the likelihood of substantially unjust administration of a policy has the effect of making it wrong to adopt that policy. I say "substantially" here in order to make clear that I do not claim that every, even the slightest, injustice has this effect. Given the inevitability of human error, some miscarriages of justice are inevitable in implementing any policy. Thus, I shall say that in situations in which we have reason to expect that a policy will be administered with *substantial* injustice, then that policy will likely be unjust *in practice,* and in situations in which there is not reason to believe that all alternative policies will be worse, it would be wrong to adopt a policy that is likely to be unjust *in practice* even if it was just *in principle.*

In section II, I argued that the death penalty was a just punishment for at least some murders. But that argument was made without reference to the actual way in which the death penalty is likely to be meted out in current-day America. Consequently, the argument proves that the death penalty is a just punishment for murder in principle. I shall now argue that when we apply the standard of justice implicit in that argument to the actual ways in which the death penalty is likely to be imposed in America today and into the foreseeable future, we find that instituting the death penalty in current-day America is unjust in practice.

When I argued that death is just punishment for murder according to the *lex talionis,* I indicated that this justification can be rightly applied only when its implied preconditions are satisfied. What are these preconditions? First, the retributive justification of the death penalty that I have defended depends on the penalty's capacity to affirm or act out the equal worth of persons. Hence a precondition of punishing justly as retribution is that the state punish in a way that treats persons as of equal worth. Second, the death penalty affirms the equal worth of persons only on the assumption that the murderer is wholly responsible for his or her crime. This is a necessary precondition of the moral legitimacy of asking him or her to pay the whole price of the harm he or she has caused, namely, a life for a life.[75] Hence a precondition of executing murderers justly as retribution is that neither the state nor the society it represents bears responsibility for what murderers have done. And third, the death penalty is a just punishment for murder according to the *lex talionis* only if the death penalty imposes a harm on the murderer roughly equivalent to the harm the murderer caused his victim. Consequently, a precondition of executing murderers justly as retribution for murder is that the death penalty be imposed without being accompanied by other harms to the murderer that make the penalty substantially worse than murder itself. Insofar as the state violates any of these preconditions of the retributive justice of the death penalty, it does injustice in practice (according to the very standard of justice by which the death penalty is justified) and, thereby, loses its right to justify its executions retributively. In this sense, a theory of the moral justification of punishment is also a theory of the moral conditions that the state must satisfy to have the right to punish.

In the remainder of this section, I shall present four ways in which the administration of the death penalty in America, currently and into the foreseeable future, violates one or more of the above-mentioned preconditions. All of these are reasons why the death penalty, justified in principle retributively, will be unjust in practice according to the very values underlying that retributive justification. I shall close the section with briefer arguments that reach the same conclusion about the death penalty justified in principle by fairness and deterrence. With that, my argument against the death penalty will be complete.

1. Discrimination in the Application of the Death Penalty among Convicted Murderers

A long line of researchers has found that, among equally guilty murderers, the death penalty is more likely to be given to blacks than to whites

---

75. Note that my claim here is a moral claim, not a legal one. The law often holds several people wholly responsible for the same act. On the other hand, the law calls for reducing responsibility under conditions of duress and, in entrapment, the law calls for eliminating culpability entirely where the state plays a role in making a crime more attractive.

and to poor defendants than to well-off ones. Though discrimination was one of the grounds upon which death penalty statutes were ruled unconstitutional in *Furman v Georgia* in 1972, there is strong evidence that it remains in the sentencing procedures ruled constitutional four years later in *Gregg v Georgia*: "Among killers of whites [in Florida], blacks are five times more likely than whites to be sentenced to death."[76] This pattern of discrimination was also evidenced, though in less pronounced form, in Texas, Ohio, and Georgia. More recently, studies have presented evidence for discrimination among convicted murderers on the basis of the race of their victims, with killers of whites standing a considerably larger chance of being sentenced to death than killers of blacks.[77] Since 1976, 82 percent of the murder victims in cases that resulted in executions were white, though whites are victims in less than half the murders committed in the United States. Of persons executed for interracial murders since 1976, four were whites who killed blacks, eighty-four were blacks who killed whites. Supreme Court Justice Harry Blackmun, who voted *for* the death penalty in 1972 and 1976, said in a 1994 dissent: "Even under the most sophisticated death penalty statutes, race continues to play a major role in determining who shall live and who shall die."[78]

---

76. W. J. Bowers and G. L. Pierce, "Racial Discrimination and Criminal Homicide under Post-*Furman* Capital Statutes," in *The Death Penalty in America*, 3rd ed., ed. Hugo A. Bedau (New York: Oxford University Press, 1982), 210, 211.

77. See D. Baldus, C. Pulaski, and G. Woodworth, *Equal Justice and the Death Penalty* (Boston: Northeastern University Press, 1990). Their study was the basis of the most recent (and unsuccessful) major constitutional challenge to the death penalty based on racial discrimination, namely, *McCleskey v Kemp*, 753 F2d 877 (1987). For other studies that reveal discrimination in capital sentencing based on race of victim, see R. Paternoster, "Race of Victim and Location of Crime: The Decision to Seek the Death Penalty in South Carolina," *Journal of Criminal Law and Criminology* 74, no. 3 (1983): 754–88; R. Paternoster, "Prosecutorial Discretion in Requesting the Death Penalty: A Case of Victim-Based Racial Discrimination," *Law and Society Review* 18 (1984): 437–78; S. Gross and R. Mauro, "Patterns of Death: An Analysis of Racial Disparities in Capital Sentencing and Homicide Victimization," *Stanford Law Review* 37 (1984): 27–120; Michael L. Radelet and Glenn L. Pierce, "Race and Prosecutorial Discretion in Homicide Cases," *Law and Society Review* 19 (1985): 587, 615-19.

78. Justice Harry Blackmun, dissenting from denial of certiorari, *Callins v Collins*, 114 US 1127, 1135 (1994). See also Richard C. Dieter, *Twenty Years of Capital Punishment: A Re-evaluation*, report by the Death Penalty Information Center [Washington, DC: June 1996], 4. Michael Radelet reviewed records of

It should be clear that a society that adopts the death penalty when it is likely to be applied in this way chooses to bring about injustice. Any society that punishes in such a discriminatory fashion loses the right to appeal to the retributive justification of the death penalty defended earlier. That justification depends on the penalty's affirmation of the equal worth of persons, and a society that reserves the death penalty for murderers coming from certain racial and socioeconomic groups clearly treats these people as of less worth than others. Likewise, a society that reserves the death penalty for the killers of whites but not of blacks treats blacks as of less worth than whites.

2. Discrimination in the Definition of Murder

Those acts that the law calls "murder" are by no means the only ways that people kill their fellow citizens in America. There is, for example, considerable evidence that many more Americans die as a result of diseases caused by preventable conditions in the workplace (toxic chemicals, coal and textile dust, etc.) than die at the hands of the murderers who show up in arrest and conviction records or on death row.[79] In 1985, three corporate executives were found guilty of murder and sentenced to twenty-five years in prison for the death of an employee that was caused by exposure to hydrogen cyanide in a film reprocessing plant.[80] The executives, it was held, knew fully the dangerousness of the situation and failed to warn their employees. Most interesting for our purposes is that this was recognized as *the first case of its kind*. The uniqueness of this case and its outcome testify that general practice is to ignore or treat lightly the subjection of workers to lethal hazards on the job.

15,978 American executions since 1739, and found thirty cases—two-tenths of 1 percent of executions!—in which a white was executed for a crime against a black. In ten of these cases, the victim was a black slave (a white man's property), and in five more, the occupational status of the black victim was higher than that of the white assailant (Michael L. Radelet, "Executions of Whites for Crimes against Blacks: Exceptions to the Rule?" *Sociological Quarterly* 30, no. 4 [1989]: 529–44).

79. Jeffrey Reiman, *The Rich Get Richer and the Poor Get Prison: Ideology, Class, and Criminal Justice*, 5th ed. (Needham Heights, MA: Allyn & Bacon, 1998), 71–78.

80. *Facts on File* (New York: Facts on File, 1985), 495.

It might be thought unfair to class such things as the failure to remove deadly occupational hazards as murder because this failure is not an act intentionally aimed at ending life. However, many state homicide statutes categorize unintended deaths caused by extreme recklessness as murder.[81] Thus, if loss of life is among the foreseeable likely consequences of failure to remove occupational hazards, as long as the victims have not freely and knowingly consented to put themselves at risk, the individual responsible for this failure ought to be held responsible for (at least) reckless homicide, and possibly murder, regardless of the particular outcome he hoped for when he acted.

It is reasonable to assume that there is some ordinary level of risk that is accepted by all members of society as an implicit condition of enjoying the benefits of progress, and of course there are some cases in which workers can be said to have freely and knowingly consented to risk the special occupational hazards that accompany their jobs; but there are as well a large number of cases in which individuals taking hazardous jobs had no realistic alternative and a large number of cases in which extraordinary hazards were known only to management—and concealed. Consider, for example, the Manville (formerly Johns Manville) asbestos case. It is predicted that 240,000 Americans who have worked with asbestos will die from asbestos-related cancer in the next thirty years. Documents made public during congressional hearings in 1979 show "that Manville and other companies within the asbestos industry covered up and failed to warn millions of Americans of the dangers associated with the fireproof, indestructible insulating fiber."[82] An article in the *American Journal of Public Health* attributes thousands of deaths to the cover-up.[83] In cases like these, employees can hardly be held to have freely put themselves at risk.

There is also evidence that the number of people who die from other practices not normally treated as murder, such as performance of unnecessary surgery and prescription of unneeded drugs, is higher than the num-

---

81. Nancy Frank, "Unintended Murder and Corporate Risk-Taking: Defining the Concept of Justifiability," *Journal of Criminal Justice* 16 (1988): 18.

82. Russell Mokhiber, *Corporate Crime and Violence: Big Business Power and the Abuse of Public Trust* (San Francisco: Sierra Club, 1988), 278, 285.

83. David E. Lilienfeld, "The Silence: The Asbestos Industry and Early Occupational Cancer Research—A Case Study," *American Journal of Public Health* 81, no. 6 (June 1991): 791.

ber of reported murder victims. And these examples can be multiplied. Moreover, the difference between the kinds of killings that are treated as murder and the kinds that are not is not an arbitrary or haphazard difference; it is a systematic identification of the ways that poor people kill as "murder" and the ways that well-off people kill as something else: "disasters," "social costs of progress," or "regulatory violations" at worst.[84]

If in our society murder is not the intentional taking of life, but the intentional taking of life *by poor people*, this has quite the same moral effect as the first sort of discrimination. It treats well-off killers as of greater worth than poor killers, and it supports the presumption that in our society murderers are not punished because they are murderers, but because they are poor. Then, adoption of the death penalty in practice amounts to instituting unjust discriminatory treatment of the poor. And this disqualifies the society from claiming that it is executing murderers to pay them in kind for their crimes and to affirm the equal worth of human beings.

3. Discrimination in the Recruitment of Murderers

The first two sorts of discrimination just considered are built into the criminal justice system; the sort that I shall now take up is arguably built into the structure of the society that that criminal justice system protects. That the death rows of our nation are populated primarily by poor people is not only the result of discriminatory sentencing. In large measure, it is the result of the fact that murder, or at least what we call murder, is done primarily by people at the bottom of society. "In the case of homicide, the empirical evidence indicates that poverty and poor economic conditions are systematically related to higher levels of homicide."[85] One confirmation of the link between poverty and homicide is that "[a]bout ninety percent of those facing capital charges cannot afford their own lawyer."[86]

---

84. Reiman, *The Rich Get Richer*, 78–81; see also 51–53.
85. Richard M. McGahey, "Dr. Ehrlich's Magic Bullet: Economic Theory, Econometrics, and the Death Penalty," *Crime and Delinquency* 26, no. 4 (October 1980): 502. Some of that evidence can be found in Peter Passell, "The Deterrent Effect of the Death Penalty: A Statistical Test," *Stanford Law Review* (November 1975): 61–80.
86. R. Tabak and M. Lane, "The Execution of Injustice: A Cost and Lack-of-Benefit Analysis of the Death Penalty," *Loyola of Los Angeles Law Review* 23 (1989): 59, 70, cited in Dieter, *Twenty Years of Capital Punishment*, 5. The quality

If people are subjected to remediable unjust social circumstances be-yond their control, and if harmful actions are a predictable response to those conditions, then those who benefit from the unjust conditions and refuse to remedy them share responsibility for the harmful acts—and thus neither the doing nor the cost of those acts can be assigned fully to the offenders alone. For example, if a slave kills an innocent person while mak-ing his escape, at least part of the blame for the killing must fall on those who have enslaved him. And this is because slavery is unjust, not merely because the desire to escape from slavery is understandable. The desire to escape from prison is understandable as well, but if the imprisonment were a just sentence, then we would hold the prisoner, and not his keepers, responsible if he killed someone while escaping. Consequently, if poverty in America is unjust, and if murder is a predictable result of this unjust poverty, then the society that refuses to remedy this poverty bears some responsibility for the murders that result.

The author of a study of the distribution of wealth in America from colonial times to the present concludes that "at no time has the majority of the U.S. adult population or households managed to gain title to any more than about ten percent of the nation's wealth."[87] This distribution of wealth is unjust in light of all of the currently popular theories of justice: *utilitarianism* (given the relative numbers of rich and poor in America, as well as the principle of declining marginal returns, redistribution could make the poor happier without an offsetting loss in happiness among the rich), or John Rawls's theory of *justice as fairness* (the worst-off shares in our society could still be increased, so the difference principle is not yet satisfied), or Robert Nozick's *libertarianism* (the original acquisition of property in America was marked by the use of force against Native Ameri-

---

of legal aid received by these indigent capital defendants is woefully bad and, due to cuts in funding, getting worse. A 1993 study by the American Bar Association "found the whole system of indigent defense to be in a state of crisis, citing a long history of warnings on this problem. In particular, it noted that death penalty defendants have been hardest hit by inadequate funding" (Richard Dieter, *With Justice for Few: The Growing Crisis in Death Penalty Representation*, report by the Death Penalty Information Center [Washington, DC: October 1995], 20 [report-ing the findings of R. Klein and R. Spangenberg, *The Indigent Defense Crisis*, prepared for the ABA Section of Criminal Justice Ad Hoc Committee on the Indi-gent Defense Crisis, 1993]).

87. Carole Shammas, "A New Look at Long-Term Trends in Wealth Inequality in the United States," *American Historical Review* 98, no. 2 (April 1993): 421.

cans and blacks, from which both groups still suffer).[88] However, given the legacies of slavery and Jim Crow; the fact of widespread discrimination based on race, religion, and gender; and the vast differences in educational opportunity facing people of different economic statuses; it hardly takes sophisticated philosophical analysis to conclude that America's lopsided distribution of wealth is unjust.

Since there is reason to believe that the vast majority of murders in America are a predictable response to the frustrations and disabilities of impoverished social circumstances, and that that impoverishment is a remediable injustice from which others in America benefit, American society bears some of the responsibility for these murders and thus has no right to exact the full cost of murders from its murderers until America has done everything possible to rectify the conditions that produce their crimes.

Van den Haag notes the connection between crime and poverty, and he explains it and its implications as follows: "Poverty does not compel crime; it only makes it more tempting."[89] And it is not absolute poverty that makes crime more tempting, only relative deprivation, the fact that some have less than others.[90] In support of this, van den Haag marshals data showing that, over the years, crime has risen along with the standard of living at the bottom of society. Since, unlike absolute deprivation, relative deprivation will be with us no matter how rich we all become as long as some have more than others, he concludes that this condition that increases the temptation to crime is just an ineradicable fact of social life, best dealt with by giving people strong incentives to resist the temptation.

This argument is flawed in several ways. First, the claim that crime is connected with poverty ought not to be simplistically interpreted as meaning that a low absolute standard of living itself causes crime. Rather, what seems to be linked to crime is the general breakdown of stable communities, institutions, and families, such as has occurred in our cities in recent decades as a result of economic and demographic trends largely out of individuals' control. Of this breakdown, poverty is today a sign and a cause, in that poverty leaves people with few defenses against the breakdown and few avenues of escape from it. It is this general breakdown that

---

88. See John Rawls, *A Theory of Justice*; and Robert Nozick, *Anarchy, State, and Utopia* (New York: Basic Books, 1974). For an extended discussion of these theories of justice, see Reiman, *Justice and Modern Moral Philosophy*.

89. Van den Haag and Conrad, *The Death Penalty*, 207.

90. Ibid., 115.

spawns crime. And this claim is quite compatible with finding that people who have lower absolute standards of living, but who dwell in more stable social surroundings with traditional institutions still intact, have lower crime rates than contemporary poor people who have higher absolute standards of living. Second, the implication of the link between poverty and crime is not simply that it is relative deprivation that tempts people to commit crime, for if that were the case, the middle class would be stealing as much from the rich as the poor do from the middle class. That this is not the case suggests that there is some threshold after which crime is no longer so tempting, and while this threshold changes historically, it is in principle one all could reach. Thus, it is not merely the (supposedly ineradicable) fact of having less than others that makes crime so tempting. Finally, everything is altered if the temptation to crime is the result, not of an ineradicable social fact, but of an injustice that can be remedied or relieved.

Insofar as we as a society tolerate the existence of remediable unjust social conditions that make crime a more reasonable alternative for a specific segment of society than for other segments, we are accomplices in the crimes that quite predictably result. As such, we lose the right to extract the full price from the criminal, and this means we lose the right to take the murderer's life in return for the life he has taken. Since the vast majority of murderers will come from the bottom of society, adopting the death penalty as their punishment imposes more harm on them than they have earned—and that means that adopting the death penalty in practice amounts to bringing about injustice.

4. Life on Death Row as Torture

The argument that the person condemned to be executed lives a life of torture stems from Albert Camus.[91] Recently, this argument has been fleshed out in fuller psychological detail by Robert Johnson, who, in his book *Condemned to Die*, recounts the painful psychological deterioration suffered by a substantial majority of the death row prisoners he studied.[92] Since the death row inmate faces execution, he is viewed as having nothing

---

91. See note 67 above and accompanying text.
92. Robert Johnson, *Condemned to Die: Life under Sentence of Death* (New York: Elsevier, 1981), 129ff.

to lose and thus treated as the most dangerous of criminals. As a result, his confinement and isolation are nearly total. Since he has no future for which to be rehabilitated, he receives the least and the worst of the prison's facilities. Since his guards know they are essentially warehousing him until his death, they treat him as something less than human—and so he is brutalized, taunted, powerless and constantly reminded of it. The result of this confinement, as Johnson reports it, is quite literally the breaking down of the structures of the ego—a process not unlike that caused by brainwashing. Since we do not reserve the term "torture" only for processes resulting in physical pain, but recognize processes that result in extreme psychological suffering as torture as well (consider sleep deprivation or the so-called Chinese water torture), Johnson's application of this term to the conditions of death row confinement seems reasonable.

It might be objected that some of the responsibility for the torturous life of death row inmates must be attributed to the inmates themselves, since in pressing their legal appeals, they delay their executions and thus prolong their time on death row. However, the unusually high rate at which capital murder convictions and sentences are reversed on appeal (estimated at nearly ten times the rate of reversals in noncapital cases; roughly half of all capital cases in the 1980s were reversed on appeal) strongly supports the idea that such appeals are necessary to test the legality of murder convictions and death penalty sentences.[93] To hold the inmate somehow responsible for the delays that result from his appeals, and thus for the (increased) torment he suffers as a consequence, is effectively to confront him with the choice of accepting execution before its legality is fully tested or suffering torture until it is. Since no just society should expect (or even want) a person to accept a sentence until its legal validity has been established, it is unjust to torture him until it has and perverse to assert that he has brought the torture on himself by his insistence that the legality of his sentence be fully tested before it is carried out.

Although it is possible that the worst features of death row might be ameliorated, it is not at all clear that its torturous nature is ever likely to be eliminated, or even that it is possible to eliminate it. In order to protect themselves against natural, painful, and ambivalent feelings of sympathy for a person awaiting a humanly inflicted death, it may be psychologically

---

93. See Costanzo and White, "An Overview of the Death Penalty," 12–14; see also Bedau, ed., *Death Penalty in America*, 243.

necessary for the guards who oversee a condemned person to think of him as less than human and treat him as such. Johnson writes: "I think it can also be argued . . . that humane death rows will not be achieved in practice because the purpose of death row confinement is to facilitate executions by dehumanizing both the prisoners and (to a lesser degree) their executioners and thus make it easier for both to conform to the etiquette of ritual killing."[94]

If conditions on death row are and are likely to continue to be a real form of psychological torture, what are the implications for the justice of the death penalty in practice? One must admit that it is no longer merely a penalty of death—it is now a penalty of torture until death. And if this is so, then it can no longer be thought of as an amount of suffering equal to that imposed by the murderer, leaving aside those murderers who have tortured their victims. Thus, at least for ordinary murderers, the death penalty would exceed the suffering they had caused and could not be justified on the retributivist basis defended above. As to whether it would be justified retribution for murderers who had tortured their victims, perhaps it would, but probably not for many. The reason is that as we move away from common instrumental murders to the pointlessly cruel ones, we move at the same time toward offenders who are more likely to be sociopaths and less likely to be fully in control of their actions in the way that legitimates retributive punishment.

My primary concern in this section has been to demonstrate that the same moral considerations that show *lex talionis* to be a just standard of desert—in particular, the recognition and affirmation of the equal worth of all persons—show as well that it would be unjust to institute the death penalty in America, in light of how it is likely to be carried out. I shall only briefly suggest how similar arguments might be made about the other two punishment rationales discussed earlier, fairness and deterrence.

Jeffrie Murphy considers the applicability of the fairness rationale to the punishment of the typical criminals in present-day American society. Writes Murphy,

The retributive theory really presupposes . . . a "gentlemen's club" picture of . . . society. . . . The rules benefit all concerned and, as a kind of debt for the benefits derived, each man owes obedience to the rules. In the absence

---

94. Robert Johnson, personal correspondence to author.

of such obedience, he deserves punishment in the sense that he owes payment for the benefits. . . . But to think that [this picture] applies to the typical criminal, from the poorer classes, is to live in a world of social and political fantasy. . . . [Such criminals] certainly would be hard-pressed to name the benefits for which they are supposed to owe obedience.[95]

Poor people are deprived of the material benefits of cooperation, and the frequent result of this is that they are deprived of the security benefits as well, inasmuch as they have little choice but to live in crime-ridden neighborhoods, where police are at best able to keep violence from getting out of hand and barely able to provide real protection for all citizens. Insofar as the benefits of obeying the law are not distributed equally to all, neither is the duty to obey, nor the debt incurred for disobeying, the same for all. Consequently, while punishment may be justified in principle for taking unfair advantage, instituting such punishment in an unjust society is unjust in practice according to the values underlying the fairness view: It punishes people for defaulting on payment for benefits they haven't received.

Since deterrence is an extension of the right of self-defense, it does not turn on notions of equal worth or personal responsibility. One is morally permitted to kill a homicidal maniac in self-defense, even though there is no assertion that he is responsible for his acts or that killing him affirms anything about his worth compared to anyone else's. Thus, even if the above-considered unjust conditions obtain, our society might still avail itself of the deterrence justification—even an unjust society has the right to defend its innocent members against harm.

But if we revert to the deterrence justification, two things must be borne in mind. First, as I argued above, we do not have reason to believe that capital punishment has a greater deterrent impact on murder than less harsh penalties. Thus, deterrence does not now justify the death penalty. Second, since the deterrence approach justifies a penalty as the least harsh means necessary to produce the obtainable level of deterrence, it can be invoked for any given punishment only if no less harsh means will produce the same deterrent effect. But there is no reason to limit the means under consideration to punishments. To use the deterrence approach to justify punishment, one must have exhausted all the ways of preventing crime

---

95. Jeffrie Murphy, "Marxism and Retribution," in *Punishment*, ed. Simmons et al., 26.

that are less harsh than punishment, in order to show that only some form of punishment is the least harsh means to deter crime. This implies that, in order to appeal to the deterrence justification for punishment, we must already have tried to eliminate crime by such nonpunitive means as eliminating the conditions like poverty that cause crime. Until we do this, our appeals to deterrence—even if valid in principle—will ring just as hollow in practice as do our appeals to retribution.

It may be objected that the various injustices catalogued in this section characterize the imposition of prison sentences as well as the death penalty, and, thus, if those injustices are grounds for abolishing the death penalty, then they are equally grounds for abolishing imprisonment. However, recall that I maintained that the injustice of a policy would not necessarily count against instituting that policy if all feasible alternatives were worse. Since I have already given arguments for preferring imprisonment to executions, and since injustice in the imposition of a milder penalty is a milder injustice than injustice in the imposition of a harsher penalty, eliminating the death penalty and limiting our punishments to imprisonment with its injustices is not worse, and is arguably better, than maintaining the death penalty with its injustices. Moreover, if, as we commonly suppose, some kind of imprisonment is needed for our criminal justice system to provide what protection and justice it can, then abolishing imprisonment is a worse alternative than maintaining it. Nothing in my argument, then, implies that we should abolish imprisonment.

I conclude that it is wrong to maintain the death penalty in practice in the United States as punishment for murder—although the penalty itself is in principle a just punishment for murder. And since I have earlier shown that it would be good to punish murder with less harsh penalties than death, I think I have shown that it is morally right in principle and in practice to abolish the death penalty in America.

3

Reply to Jeffrey Reiman

Louis P. Pojman

In his perspicacious and challenging essay "Why the Death Penalty Should be Abolished in America"[1] Jeffrey Reiman qualifiedly accepts the two claims in favor of executing murderers: retributivism and deterrence. Regarding retributivism, he says, some murderers deserve the death penalty. Regarding deterrence, he says, "if the death penalty were needed to deter future murders, it would be unjust to future victims not to impose it." Then he argues five points:

1. Although the death penalty is a just punishment for some murderers, "it is not unjust to punish murderers less harshly (down to a certain limit)."
2. We have "no good reason to believe that the death penalty is needed to deter future murders."
3. In "refraining from imposing the death penalty, the state, by its vivid and impressive example, contributes to reducing our tolerance for cruelty and thereby fosters the advance of human civilization as we understand it."
4. Conclusion: Theses 1 to 3, taken together, "imply that we do no injustice to actual or potential murder victims, and we do some considerable good, in refraining from executing murders."

---

1. Reiman's essay is one of the clearest, most cogent expressions for abolitionism that I have read, and I appreciate the careful judiciousness of his reasoning. Note that while we come to radically different conclusions, we agree on many essential points. We are both retributivist, holding to a strong notion of justice as desert. We both acknowledge that just desert would in principle permit torturing the torturer. I'm especially impressed by Reiman's ambitious attempt to bring several principles of punishment into a unity.

133

Louis P. Pojman

5. This conclusion (Thesis 4) is reinforced by the fact that, "though the death penalty is *in principle* a just penalty for murder, it is unjust *in practice* in America because it is applied in arbitrary and discriminatory ways and this is likely to continue into the foreseeable future."

Regarding thesis 1, unlike many abolitionists who argue that the death penalty is unjust in principle, Reiman is a retributivist as I am, holding that the guilty deserve to be punished. The difference between us is that I hold that we ought to punish the guilty with a penalty equivalent to the harm caused or the wrong done, which he denies. He writes, "the fact that a punishment is justly deserved does not, in my view, entail that someone has a duty to impose that punishment. Rather, ... desert creates *a right to punish,* not a duty to do so." I hold that justice consists in giving people what they deserve, so that there is a duty to impose the death penalty on some murderers, even if it is only a prima facie duty, which may be overridden by other moral concerns. Regarding thesis 2, Reiman accepts that if the death penalty were needed to deter future murders, he would favor it. But he and I disagree on whether it is needed to deter future murders. Regarding thesis 3, Reiman holds that turning away from the death penalty will help civilize our society. I am doubtful here and will argue against this point. Thesis 4, of course, follows from 1 to 3, so I will reject it, since I reject thesis 2 and 3. Regarding thesis 5, that the application of the death penalty is arbitrary and discriminatory, *so we should abandon its use,* I am skeptical. We should reform our system but not abandon the use of the death penalty. I will argue, contrary to Reiman: (1) That justice as desert creates duties to give people what they deserve; (2) that the death penalty is needed as a deterrence; (3) that abolishing the death penalty at this time does not promote civilization; and (4) that the "fact" that the application of the death penalty is sometimes arbitrary and discriminatory in America does not warrant our abolishing the institution in America.

Does Justice as Desert Create Duties?

Reiman holds that some murderers deserve the punishment of the death penalty but that we have no duty to punish them this way. If I understand him, he and I agree that the State has a *right* to punish the guilty in proportion to the gravity of their crime, which may include executing the murderer. Although granting the State this right is sufficient to establish the permissibility of capital punishment in some cases, it will make the retentionist's case stronger if one can defend the thesis that society has a duty to execute those who kill with malice aforethought. I hold that desert creates a *prima facie* duty to punish with a harm equivalent to the crime. In Part I of my essay I developed an argument along the following lines:

1. Justice, as giving people what they deserve, consists in rewarding the good according to their virtue and the bad according to their vice.
2. We ought to be just, whenever we can. This includes having laws to promote justice.
3. Therefore, we ought to institute laws and legal procedures to punish the guilty according to their vice (i.e., according to the evil they have intentionally done).

   My principle (DD = "desert creates duties") of treating (rewarding or punishing) people according to their desert can be formulated this way: Let S = the subject, and x = the treatment (good or bad treatment):

   DD: If S deserves x, and you are in a position to give S x, and no moral reason overrides or neutralizes giving S x, then you have a duty to give S x.

Perhaps the formula needs to be qualified. If others are in an even better position to give S x or if S specifically deserves to get x from someone else, you may not have a duty to give S x. I will assume that the qualifications will not affect the central point that someone's deserving treatment of various kinds creates an obligation on others to give that person what he or she deserves. A neutralizing reason may include the fact that we simply don't know that someone deserves some reward and punishment, so that we are not required to give him what he deserves.

As I noted, mitigating circumstances, overriding duties (including the duty to err on the side of mercy), and practical considerations may offset this prima facie duty. While we may have a general duty to benevolence, to come to the aid of anyone who deserves to be helped, special obligations to our family, friends, and community may override that general duty to benevolence. Similarly, our duty to punish the guilty according to their deserts may be overridden by other obligations. Because we have judicial procedures which have been instituted to carry out justice, we may not take the "law into our own hands" as it were, but ought to follow due process, even when it yields unjust results in individual cases. Similarly, while the torturer may deserve to be tortured, our duty to give him what he strictly deserves may be offset by considerations of mercy, existing cultural practices, utility, or simply because the personal (e.g., psychological) costs in carrying out torture are unacceptable. Nonetheless, desert has normative force, creating an obligation to give people what they deserve. We intuitively sense this when we object that an employer is exploiting workers by paying them far less than they deserve. Cheating and stealing are kinds of undeserved acquisitions of goods. The person who is not grateful to his benefactor, who does not sense an obligation to reciprocate for services rendered, lacks a moral virtue. Desert claims are normative, as reflected in the Hindu and Buddhist doctrine of karma (people deserve the fruits of their deeds—whatsoever a man sows that shall he reap), in the Judeo-Christian idea of divine judgment (God rewards the good with life in heaven and the evil with life in hell), in Kant's idea that people ought to flourish or suffer equivalent to their virtue or vice, and in Marx's Labor Theory of Value (that the entrepreneur ought to give the worker what he deserves, so that not to do so is a kind of theft). I confess it is intuitively self-evident that the good deserve to prosper and the evil to suffer—until they repent—and that in an ideal universe the virtuous and vicious would get what they deserve. Those harmed through no fault of their own would be compensated. Even though we obviously cannot bring this state of justice about in our universe, isn't part of our duty to try to do so whenever feasible? Don't we have some basic duty to reward and punish according to deserts, when we have the ability to do so and have some idea of what people do deserve?

Note that Reiman objects to a version of theorem DD, but offers no argument against it except three alleged counter-examples.

> I present here three compelling claims that support the view that desert does not entail a duty to give what is deserved: First, the victim of an offense has the right to forgive the offending party rather than punish him though he deserves to be punished; second, we have no duty (not even a prima facie duty) to torture torturers even if they deserve to be tortured; and third, though great benefactors of humanity deserve to be rewarded, no one necessarily has a duty to provide that reward.

These counterexamples certainly should give us pause, but, we may ask, Do any of these counterexamples actually undermine DD? Let's examine them in order.

(1) The right to forgive the offender shows that we don't have a duty to give what is deserved. To evaluate this claim we need to understand what forgiveness is. I follow Bishop Joseph Butler in defining forgiveness as the "forswearing of resentment."[2] If this is so, then I can forgive someone without withdrawing the requirement of punishment. Suppose I am abused, raped and robbed by a close relative. I may forgive him his deeds but still believe he should accept the penalties enjoined by our legal system. Furthermore, it may be inappropriate or immoral to forgive him if he feels no remorse and has not repented of the evil he has done to me. My forgiving him may depict a vice in me, a lack of sufficient self-respect. The concept of forgiveness seems to work best where there is repentance on the part of the offender, though utilitarian reasons may also be operative. But suppose you want to go further than this and agree with Reiman that the offended person has a right to forgive the offender in a manner that enjoins removing the penalty which he deserves. This does not necessarily count against DD, for we could still say that the prima facie duty to give people what they deserve can be overridden by our right to forgive and show mercy. The point is that the offended person has no duty to forgive an unrepentant offender, so that the prima facie obligation persists until it is overridden.

(2) Reiman's second claim is that "we have no duty (not even a prima facie duty) to torture torturers even if they deserve to be tortured." But isn't the correct assessment that we do have a prima facie duty to bring it about that the torturer is punished in kind but that other moral considerations may override this duty? The social costs to torturing the torturer may be too high. I may be psychologically brutalized by torturing the offender. Here a certain benign cultural relativity may prevail, so that in some cultures a general revulsion will be directed at the practice of torture, whereas in others it will not. The practice cannot be viewed in isolation from the whole fabric of a culture. Furthermore, the torturer may not deserve to be tortured, but he may deserve some different (lesser or greater) punishment. If his deed was done under social pressure (say, a Nazi prison guard

---

2. Joseph Butler, *Fifteen Sermons* (London, 1726), Sermon 8 "Upon Resentment" and Sermon 9 "Upon Forgiveness and Injuries." My views have been influenced by the discussion of Jeffrie Murphy and Jean Hampton in their book, *Forgiveness and Mercy* (Cambridge University Press, 1988) and by Tziporah Kasachkoff.

who is following orders by torturing a prisoner), he may deserve severe punishment, but it may not require us to torture him.

Note that Reiman sometime writes as though he recognizes the prima facie duty to give the torturer what he deserves:

> When, however, we refrain from raping rapists or torturing torturers, we do so for reasons of morality, not of practicality. And, given the justice of the *lex talionis*, these moral reasons cannot amount to claiming that it would be unjust to rape rapists or torture torturers. Rather, the claim must be that, even though it would be just to rape rapists and torture torturers, other moral considerations weigh against doing so.

But isn't this exactly what DD asserts? We have a prima facie duty to do justice, justice might require us to torture the torturer. But other moral reasons override this prima facie duty. To continue to reject DD Reiman would have argue that justice imposes no obligations on us, which seems to remove justice from the sphere of morality as a definite principle. I don't think he wants to do this.

(3) Reiman's third counterexample is the claim that no one necessarily has a duty to provide a reward to a great benefactor of society. Once again, my principle would enjoin a prima facie duty for society to provide the benefactor with an appropriate reward, but there may be other moral grounds that override this, for "no one necessarily has a duty to provide that reward." My inclination is to say that we go astray when we think that financial rewards are the only way to give benefactors what they deserve. What they deserve is gratitude, admiration, respect, and perhaps special consideration in having their needs met before those of others. How should we reward Mother Teresa for the enormous good she has done for others? One might ask her. Actually, my wife and I did ask her, while visiting her in Calcutta in 1990. She said that the way we could honor her would be by carrying out the spirit of her programs, in helping orphans, the poor, and the unborn (supporting the right-to-life movement). Perhaps some would have moral reservations about the last item, but it gives us some clue as to how to reward great benefactors. Or consider a military hero, call him Sergent York, who has saved his battalion by risking his life against intense enemy fire with the result that the battalion was able to win a decisive victory in the war. Ten people, including Sgt. York are in need of an organ (say a liver transplant), and none of the other

candidates' service to society is as great as his. Might it not be the case that we have a prima facie duty to give the scarce organ to him?

I conclude this discussion in defense of DD. We do have a prima facie duty to give people what they deserve. Justice requires it.

2. Is the Death Penalty Needed in Order to Deter Future Murders?

I have already discussed this point in Part II of my essay defending the death penalty, so I will be brief here. Reiman, in arguing that the death penalty doesn't deter (any better than long-term prison sentences) commits a common abolitionist mistake of arguing that because the sum of the sociological evidence shows no significant deterrent effect of the death penalty, the evidence supports the thesis that there *is no significant deterrent effect*. The inference is invalid, for the sociological evidence doesn't *show that there is no deterrent effect*. It doesn't show either that there is or is not a deterrent effect. It is inconclusive on the matter. One can see why. There simply are too many variables to be controlled for, including social conditions, genetic make-up, such demographical factors as age and racial distribution, law enforcement factors, knowledge of the consequences of getting caught, and opportunity factors—just to name a few broad categories. Perhaps if we experimented by executing people who committed murder on the even months but gave long prison sentences to those who committed murders on the odd months, we could come close to providing reliable data on the likelihood of the deterrent effect of the death penalty. Until we have better ways of measuring the effects of social policy, we should take the sociological evidence with a grain of salt.

Reiman doesn't deal with van den Haag's Best Bet Argument, which strikes me as sound. If we don't have hard evidence that the death penalty deters, we should bet on it saving potential murder victims rather than bet on saving the lives of the murderers. No doubt he will comment on this in his response, but since I don't know what that response is, I can only ask you to remind yourself of the argument in Part II of my essay.

Reiman is correct in arguing that the fact that one penalty is feared more than another doesn't entail that it will deter more than a less feared one. He thinks that the lack of statistical correlation for deterrence places the burden of proof on the retentionist who argues that the death penalty does deter. I argued, following recognized work in criminology, that the criminal, in planning many crimes, engages in a cost-benefit form of analysis in which he takes into consideration (if only subconsciously) the overall value of his criminal act. If the crime's pay-off is likely to be high and the chances of getting caught are low, the attractiveness of the crime is heightened; but if the penalty for the crime is lowered, the crime increases in attractiveness. Conversely, if the penalty increases, the attractiveness decreases. Long-term imprisonment without parole is likely to be, on this account, a greater deterrent than short-term imprisonment or long-term imprisonment with parole. The possibility of long-term imprisonment *plus* the possibility of the death penalty is likely to be an even greater deterrent, even as the possibility of winning the division championship plus the Super Bowl championship would be a greater incentive for a professional football team than merely the chance of winning the division championship. All things being equal, the greater the evil, the greater the deterrence, and the greater the blessing, the greater the incentive.[3] Not all murderers reason in this way, but the overall consciousness of many criminals seems to follow this pattern. Criminals often act rationally (from their point of view) in committing crimes, including the crime of murder. Furthermore, the anecdotal evidence, which I cited in Part II, cannot be dismissed as insignificant. Some criminals have transported their potential victims across borders from retentionist states to abolitionist states before they commit murder, and others have testified that they were deterred by the threat of execution. I have personal knowledge of the deterrent effect of the death penalty. Both a friend and my brother became involved in criminal activity (robbery) for a time. My friend carried a gun but kept it unloaded, while my brother wouldn't even carry a gun though it would have made his work easier. They acted as they did for fear of using it, lest they end up in the electric chair. I rest my case.

---

3. To support this point Reiman quotes David Conway in note 67 "[G]iven the choice, I would strongly prefer one thousand years in hell to eternity. Nonetheless, if one thousand years in hell were the penalty for some action, it would be quite sufficient to deter me from performing that action." The point about the threshold effect of deterrence is well taken, but it doesn't settle anything. The threat of life imprisonment probably deters many would-be criminals, but, doubtless, others would only be deterred from some crimes by a penalty as severe as death. Perhaps only the possibility of a thousand years in hell would deter other criminals.

:ny pain whatsoever—by a painless lethal injection. But is it really a good thing to eliminate pain in the punishment of murderers? Doesn't the murderer deserve some pain?

Regarding the subjugation of one person by another, Reiman writes:

> I contend that execution is especially horrible, and it is so in a way similar to (though not identical with) the way in which torture is especially horrible. I believe we view torture as especially awful because of two of its features, which also characterize execution: intense pain and the spectacle of one person being completely subject to the power of another. This latter is separate from the issue of pain, since it is something that offends us about unpainful things, such as slavery (even voluntarily entered) and prostitution (even voluntarily chosen as an occupation). Execution shares this separate feature, since killing a bound and defenseless human being enacts the total subjugation of that person to his fellows.

While we may agree that full autonomy is a good thing, there are many goods which may conflict with autonomy and override it. Here are a few: a good upbringing and education, entering a religious order, restraining violent people who either are not autonomous or use their autonomy to harm, and submitting to training which will result in higher expected personal utility. All these processes involve subjecting yourself to another. Children are in "total subjugation" to their parents. Patients undergoing surgery are in "total subjugation" to their surgeons. Education requires a great deal of subjugation to a regime and to teachers. The long-term prison sentences which Reiman advocates for murderers may involve every bit as much subjugation as slavery, perhaps more subjugation than slavery under a benign master who may have the slave's interests at heart. Parents have their children's interest at heart. Religious people wholly subjugate themselves to God or a religious authority. How is this different from voluntary slavery? Subjugation itself is not necessarily evil. It all depends on whether the limiting of freedom is morally justified, all things considered. The question is whether the prisoner, including the murderer on death row, deserves to be subjugated, deserves to have his freedom restricted. I would think Reiman believes that he does, and so I find him simply inconsistent here.

Civilville

Let me tell a story in order to illustrate my contention that although the death penalty may cause extra suffering and subjugation it may never-

3. Will Abolishing the Death Penalty at This Ti Promote Civilization in America?

Reiman argues that the death penalty is a just punishment for cei nous crimes but that it should nevertheless be eliminated on the ț that we would thereby become more civilized because the death ļ *increases pain* and *involves the total subjugation* of one person by (as does slavery and prostitution.[4] I question whether there is any nec connection between eliminating the death penalty and civilization. Fi want to challenge Reiman's two criteria for increased civilization: the ening of pain and the lessening of subjugation of people by others. I aç that, all things being equal, these are good things and may enhance civ zation, but, again, they may not. Suppose, for example, we find a way extend life, but that the unfortunate means to do so is painful surgei (many cardiac patients report such excruciating pain while undergoing an gioplasty and stent treatment). Isn't it obvious that some pain is instru-mentally good? For pain sensation may cause suitable limb and life-saving behavior, it warns us of such dangers as fire or electrical shock, and it may also enable us to empathize with others, thus making us kinder and gentler people. But, of course, we could meet Reiman's requirement for less pain while retaining the death penalty, for we can execute the criminal without

---

4. Ernest van den Haag has pointed out that these analogies fail since slavery, unlike murder, is involuntary and prostitution may be voluntary but need not in-volve the total subjugation of one person by another. Yet Reiman thinks that there is something evil about subjugation even if it is voluntary. He doesn't say what that is.

Sometimes abolitionists point out that all the other Western civilizations have abolished the death penalty, so that we are in the dubious company of South Africa and Russia in retaining it. This kind of reasoning ignores the vastly different extent of the problem of crime in the United States compared with that of Western Eu-rope, where the murder rate is often a tiny fraction of what it is here. It also assumes that the majority must be right, a position I find objectionable and in need of argument. Abolitionists always cite Europe when claiming that civilized nations must renounce capital punishment. However, one can read this trend an-other way: Perhaps they are nations dying, nations that no longer have the heart to stand up for what is right and maintain a deep sense of justice based on desert. When the good and the bad are treated equally well, when merit and individual responsibility are sacrificed for a shortsighted utility, when sentimentality replaces commitment to the good, even a good that calls on us to inflict punishment on the evil, society is on the road—not to hell—but to oblivion.

3. Will Abolishing the Death Penalty at This Time Promote Civilization in America?

Reiman argues that the death penalty is a just punishment for certain hei-nous crimes but that it should nevertheless be eliminated on the grounds that we would thereby become more civilized because the death penalty *increases pain* and *involves the total subjugation* of one person by others, as does slavery and prostitution.[4] I question whether there is any necessary connection between eliminating the death penalty and civilization. First, I want to challenge Reiman's two criteria for increased civilization: the less-ening of pain and the lessening of subjugation of people by others. I agree that, all things being equal, these are good things and may enhance civili-zation, but, again, they may not. Suppose, for example, we find a way to extend life, but that the unfortunate means to do so is painful surgery (many cardiac patients report such excruciating pain while undergoing an-gioplasty and stent treatment). Isn't it obvious that some pain is instru-mentally good? For pain sensation may cause suitable limb and life-saving behavior, it warns us of such dangers as fire or electrical shock, and it may also enable us to empathize with others, thus making us kinder and gentler people. But, of course, we could meet Reiman's requirement for less pain while retaining the death penalty, for we can execute the criminal without

---

4. Ernest van den Haag has pointed out that these analogies fail since slavery, unlike murder, is involuntary and prostitution may be voluntary but need not in-volve the total subjugation of one person by another. Yet Reiman thinks that there is something evil about subjugation even if it is voluntary. He doesn't say what that is.

Sometimes abolitionists point out that all the other Western civilizations have abolished the death penalty, so that we are in the dubious company of South Africa and Russia in retaining it. This kind of reasoning ignores the vastly different extent of the problem of crime in the United States compared with that of Western Eu-rope, where the murder rate is often a tiny fraction of what it is here. It also assumes that the majority must be right, a position I find objectionable and in need of argument. Abolitionists always cite Europe when claiming that civilized nations must renounce capital punishment. However, one can read this trend an-other way: Perhaps they are nations dying, nations that no longer have the heart to stand up for what is right and maintain a deep sense of justice based on desert. When the good and the bad are treated equally well, when merit and individual responsibility are sacrificed for a shortsighted utility, when sentimentality replaces commitment to the good, even a good that calls on us to inflict punishment on the evil, society is on the road—not to hell—but to oblivion.

any pain whatsoever—by a painless lethal injection. But is it really a good thing to eliminate pain in the punishment of murderers? Doesn't the murderer deserve some pain?

Regarding the subjugation of one person by another, Reiman writes:

> I contend that execution is especially horrible, and it is so in a way similar to (though not identical with) the way in which torture is especially horrible. I believe we view torture as especially awful because of two of its features, which also characterize execution: intense pain and the spectacle of one person being completely subject to the power of another. This latter is separate from the issue of pain, since it is something that offends us about unpainful things, such as slavery (even voluntarily entered) and prostitution (even voluntarily chosen as an occupation). Execution shares this separate feature, since killing a bound and defenseless human being enacts the total subjugation of that person to his fellows.

While we may agree that full autonomy is a good thing, there are many goods which may conflict with autonomy and override it. Here are a few: a good upbringing and education, entering a religious order, restraining violent people who either are not autonomous or use their autonomy to harm, and submitting to training which will result in higher expected personal utility. All these processes involve subjecting yourself to another. Children are in "total subjugation" to their parents. Patients undergoing surgery are in "total subjugation" to their surgeons. Education requires a great deal of subjugation to a regime and to teachers. The long-term prison sentences which Reiman advocates for murderers may involve every bit as much subjugation as slavery, perhaps more subjugation than slavery under a benign master who may have the slave's interests at heart. Parents have their children's interest at heart. Religious people wholly subjugate themselves to God or a religious authority. How is this different from voluntary slavery? Subjugation itself is not necessarily evil. It all depends on whether the limiting of freedom is morally justified, all things considered. The question is whether the prisoner, including the murderer on death row, deserves to be subjugated, deserves to have his freedom restricted. I would think Reiman believes that he does, and so I find him simply inconsistent here.

Civilville

Let me tell a story in order to illustrate my contention that although the death penalty may cause extra suffering and subjugation it may nevertheless be an ingredient of a civilized society. Civilville is a society like ours. Its laws are similar, and it has retained the death penalty. Where it is different than ours pertains to legal reform: It underwent moral and legal reform some time ago, eliminating arbitrariness in the application of the death penalty. This legal reform came about through appointing special nonpartisan panels of experts as the jurors in murder trials. The reforms eliminated much of the influence of race and wealth and encouraged the factual presentation of evidence, so that not only has the great majority of citizens come to believe in the fairness of the system but citizens have cooperated with the police and judicial system as never before in the history of Civilville. Whether or not the death penalty actually deters would-be murders is still a debatable issue, but the murder rate has gone down by virtue of citizen reporting. Because community morale is high, citizens are not hesitant to report suspicious activities, give testimony, and vote for judges and lawmakers of high integrity.

Civilville has also undergone moral reform. Its people have gradually become more sensitive to the needs of others and strive mightily to be fair. Most of the citizens are vegetarians, judging the killing of animals for food to be an unnecessary evil. They also have a low abortion rate, holding that whether or not fetuses are persons, they will, if allowed to develop in society, become persons and are, unlike criminals, innocent. The citizens are meritocrats, believing that the good should prosper and the evil should be punished, and that the most qualified people should get the best positions and the less able should be encouraged to improve themselves. Because the principle of just desert is deeply rooted in their souls, people of Civilville are retributivists who advocate that the good should be rewarded for their social contributions and criminals should be punished in proportion to the viciousness of their crimes. It's true that mercy mitigates strict justice, so they do not torture the torturer or rape the rapist (though they deserve that), but they do castrate the rapist and execute those convicted of first-degree murder.

I interviewed the people of Civilville and asked them whether they thought that substituting long prison sentences for the death penalty would make them more civilized. They admitted that while in some cases long sentences might be kinder, for the most part the death penalty for heinous crimes symbolized their meritocratic position that those who murder innocent people deserve to be executed by the State. They are perplexed by many liberals in our society who, without the slightest hesitation, advocate aborting innocent fetuses and eating innocent animals but become apoplectic about executing mass murderers. I would be proud to call myself a citizen of Civilville.

Pain, Suffering, and Progress

Reiman and I share a common concern for a just society. We are both committed to a more moral, civilized world, but we differ on the way to get there. He wants to eliminate or greatly lessen pain and physical suffering, reducing it to "reflective pain . . . that comes with comparing what is to what might have been and that can be temporarily ignored by thinking about other things." He quotes Nietzsche, that "pain did not hurt as much [in olden times] as it does today." He means that people used to tolerate pain better than they do now. My immediate questions are: How do we know this, and how is this relevant? I've heard the same argument used regarding depriving minorities and Native Americans of benefits ("they don't feel it as much as we do" or "they have a greater tolerance for pain and hardship than we do"). If people at different times can tolerate pain better than those at other times, can't people of different cultures tolerate pain better than those of others? Should we take this into consideration? If we found that some people tolerated being deprived of their rights better than other people, would our depriving them of those rights be less wrong? I doubt it, and I also doubt whether the criminal's inability to tolerate as much pain as his ancestors is a good reason for not inflicting on him the suffering he justly deserves.

Be this as it may, I too want to ameliorate *some* pain and suffering, gratuitous pain and suffering. I am against torturing people except when it will prevent a catastrophe (because of its stand against torture and for human rights, I am a member of Amnesty International), and I am a vegetarian because the wanton treatment and killing of animals, especially in animal factories, involves unnecessary cruelty. But I'm not against *all* pain and suffering. It is true that we live in an anesthetized culture where drugs are a multibillion-dollar industry. Corporal punishment is frowned upon, spanking is considered out of date, and our lives have become disembodied, centered on impersonal and abstract notions (often the products of technology, like the computer). But I'm not sure that this abstractification and anesthetization of existence is all for the good. I worry that we may be adopting a mindless Epicureanism at the expense of a Stoic ability to face hardship bravely, to resolutely endure the aches of existence for the sake of becoming stronger. Some suffering can be redemptive. Freud rejected painkillers for his pain, preferring mental lucidity with torment to a painless but dulled mind. Maybe we have become soft and flabby, fearful of the pain and suffering which are necessary or relevant to achieving civilization. If Plato is right, that nothing great was ever accomplished without great struggle and great suffering, then the elimination or inappropriate reduction of it may actually destroy civilization, bringing to pass T. S. Eliot's refrain that "the world ends not with a bang but a whimper."[5] On the contrary, being held accountable for one's deeds, may involve experiencing the suffering that accompanies our mistakes. We learn by the pain of our failures, as well as by the pleasures of our successes. They are valuable reinforcement mechanisms.

Reiman seems to advocate the abolition not only of capital punishment, but of virtually all corporal punishment. He is no doubt horrified at Singapore's practice of caning criminals, such as in the case of the caning of the American Michael Fay, who broke a Singapore law by vandalizing property with graffiti. Reiman wants to reduce all punishment to deprivation of freedom. He has quoted Nietzsche to the effect that pain hurts more in the present than it did in the past, but perhaps we should quote Nietzsche once more, this time as a commentator on Reiman's proposal to eliminate physical and mental suffering in punishment:

> There is a point in the history of society when it becomes so pathologically soft and tender that among other things it sides even with those who harm it, criminals, and does this quite seriously and honestly. Punishing somehow seems unfair to it, and it is certain that imagining "punishment" and "being supposed to punish" hurts it, arouses fear in it. "Is it not enough to render him *undangerous*? Why still punish? Punishing itself is terrible." With this question, herd morality, the morality of timidity, draws its ultimate conse-

---

5. T. S. Eliot "The Hollow Men" in *Collected Poems 1909–1962* (New York: Harcourt, Brace, Jovanovich, 1934). The poem ends:
This is the way the world ends
This is the way the world ends
This is the way the world ends
Not with a bang but a whimper.
A lot more needs to be said on the importance of suffering and struggle for civilization. I have noticed that corporal punishment has different effects on different children in the process of socialization.

quence. . . . The imperative of herd timidity: "We want that some day there should be *nothing anymore to be afraid of!*"[6]

Writing well over one hundred years ago, Nietzsche predicted that people would some day call this "progress."

4. Is the Application of the Death Penalty in America Arbitrary and Discriminatory, and If So, Does That Fact Entail That We Should Abolish It?

Reiman quotes approvingly the news report of February 3, 1997: "The American Bar Association, the nation's largest and most influential organization of lawyers . . . , voted overwhelmingly to seek a halt to the use of the death penalty, asserting that it is administered through 'a haphazard maze of unfair practices.'" I take it that this quotation is meant to lend authority to Reiman's case that the application of the death penalty in the United States is arbitrary and discriminatory. His main argument is that if the conditions for the application of a policy are unjust, the policy itself becomes unjust in practice, however just it may be in principle. I have already addressed this issue in Part II of my essay. Here I wish only to make three points.

1. There are many things wrong with our criminal justice system, and both Reiman and I and, presumably, you, the reader, deplore them and want to fix them. The American Bar Association (ABA) and Reiman have called for the suspension of all executions, arguing that the death penalty is applied arbitrarily and unfairly. This is a non sequitur.

If the ABA and Reiman wanted to make the death penalty less arbitrary and unfair, they would support measures to improve and streamline evidence gathering, trials, sentencing, appeals, and execution processes, so that punishment would be applied more fairly to all regardless of economic and educational status, gender and race. For one thing, they could provide more pro bono service for the poor than they now do. They could reform the jury system, so that more enlightened, impartial jurors were chosen instead of less capable ones. They could apply justice more consistently and swiftly. But I suspect that those ABA members who voted for a mora-

---

6. Friedrich Nietzsche, *Beyond Good and Evil*, trans. Walter Kaufmann (Random House, 1966), 114.

torium on the death penalty aren't as interested in judicial reform as they are in abolition of the death penalty. After all, whose fault is it that the criminal justice system contains "a haphazard maze of unfair practices"? Who is it that creates our laws? What group dominates Congress, whence national statutes derive? What group dominates state legislatures, whence state laws derive? What group makes up our judicial system, which carries out the laws and practices? That the American Bar Association, the official organization of lawyers, complains about a legal practice and calls on the nation to halt it is tantamount to the American Medical Association announcing that because of egregious medical malpractice in the nation doctors will refuse to treat AIDS or cancer patients.

Here is how I see the alleged arbitrary and discriminatory problem: The institution of capital punishment with regard to social functions is complex. The death penalty can be abused. It can operate in a manner that ignores mitigating circumstances, arbitrarily, and even prejudicially. The process can be corrupted so that innocent people are executed for crimes they did not commit. In this sense, the death penalty is like a fire engine. Fire engines serve a useful purpose. They are effective in putting out fires, saving property and lives. But occasionally they run over and even kill a pedestrian. This is tragic; but if only a few pedestrians are killed, we don't cease to use fire engines. But suppose that fire trucks begin to run over a lot of people, so that they become dangerous weapons, whose effectiveness is seriously compromised. In this case, we would probably decide not to use them, resorting to other means to put out fires. The same holds for capital punishment. If and when it becomes an institution producing more harm than good, we should cease to use it. But until that time, we should strive to train those who use this institution in a manner that ensures it will be used justly. It would seem that the institution is still viable and that we should do everything possible to improve and reform it.[7]

---

7. One point of contention between Reiman and myself is the issue of egalitarianism. Reiman holds that all people are of equal worth. I deny that. All people should be equal under the law and held to the same moral standards, but some people are worth more than others. For example, Mother Teresa, Mahatma Gandhi, Albert Schweitzer, Abraham Lincoln and Martin Luther King Jr. are worth more than Adolf Hitler, Joseph Stalin, Jeffrey Dahmer, Steven Judy, Ted Bundy, Timothy McVeigh and other parasites of society. Although egalitarian rhetoric pervades our culture, I suggest it is an unexamined falsehood.

Consider Smith, a man of low morals and lower intelligence, who abuses his

2. Reiman exaggerates the arbitrary and discriminatory aspect of the application of the death penalty. At least it is not clear that our system is as bad as he claims it is. As I showed in Part II the claim that blacks are penalized for crimes more than whites fails to note that blacks, especially young black males, commit proportionately far more violent crimes than whites. (Even Rev. Jesse Jackson admitted that when he was walking down city streets and heard footsteps behind him, his heart began to pound— until he looked behind him and with relief noticed that the young people were white.) Exactly who or what is ultimately responsible for this phenomenon of black violence is a difficult question, but if we are to treat black males as moral agents, we must hold them to the same standards as Asians, Hispanics, and whites. My own conviction is that by sending a message that blacks are merely victims of social oppression, we encourage irresponsible living and loss of self-respect.

3. If abolitionists like Reiman and the ABA who call for a moratorium on the death penalty in the whole of the United States really were concerned about legal reform, wouldn't they propose a policy of surveying each state's application of the death penalty? Suppose, for example, that we find that California's policy results in widespread abuse and sentencing of innocents to the death penalty, but Arizona's policy proceeds fairly. We

---

wife and children, who hates exercising or work, for whom novels are dull and art a waste of time, and whose joy it is to spend his days as a couch potato, drinking beer, while watching mud wrestling, violent sports, and soap operas on TV. He is an avid voyeur, devoted to child pornography. He is devoid of intellectual curiosity, eschews science, politics, and religion, and eats and drinks in a manner more befitting a pig than a person. Smith lacks wit, grace, humor, technical skill, ambition, courage, self-control, and wisdom. He is antisocial, morose, lazy, a freeloader who feels no guilt about living on welfare when he is perfectly able to work, has no social conscience and barely avoids getting caught for his petty thievery. He has no talents, makes no social contribution, lacks a moral sense, and from the perspective of the good of society, would be better off dead. But Smith is proud of one thing: that he is "sacred," of "infinite worth," equal in intrinsic value to Abraham Lincoln, Mother Teresa, Albert Schweitzer, the Dalai Lama, Jesus Christ, Gandhi, and Albert Einstein. He is inviolable—and proud of it—in spite of any deficiency of merit. From the egalitarian perspective, in spite of appearances to the contrary, Smith is of equal intrinsic worth as the best citizen in his community. I suggest this is the myth of liberalism, "The Emperor's New Clothes" of our culture. For a further discussion, see my article "On Equal Human Worth: A Critique of Contemporary Egalitarianism" in *Equality: Selected Readings*, ed. Louis P. Pojman and Robert Westmoreland (Oxford University Press, 1996).

could call for a moratorium on executions in California, until reforms were instituted, while retaining it in Arizona. Or we might conclude that a certain district in California applies the death penalty arbitrarily and penalize that district, but not the entire state.

Conclusion

Reiman and I agree that justice demands that some murderers deserve the death penalty, and we agree that we have a prima facie duty to impose the death penalty under certain conditions. We differ somewhat on those conditions. We also differ as to whether the death penalty deters. If I am correct, by abolishing the death penalty we make murder less costly to the criminal and put an increased number of innocent people at risk. We also differ on the relationship of the death penalty to promoting civilization. I have tried to show not only that Reiman lacks a cogent argument for any necessary or strongly contingent connection between the abolition of the death penalty and civilization, but that this institution, properly applied, may actually enhance our quest for a deeply moral society. I have argued that while our criminal justice system and society, as a whole, has injustices, the moral thing to do is to reform both the criminal justice system and society itself. We ought not throw out the baby with the dirty bathwater.

4

Reply to Louis P. Pojman

Jeffrey Reiman

Louis Pojman's essay in favor of the death penalty contains numerous accounts of grisly murders that, no doubt, evoke feelings of anger in the reader and maybe even cause the reader to want to see the murderers killed. The accounts often have this effect on me, too. However, let's be clear: Our job here is not to determine what we *feel* about murderers or what we *want* to do to them. Our job is to figure out what we *should* do, what it is *morally right* to do to murderers. For this, we must consult our reason and come up with arguments rather than feelings. I have presented my arguments against executing murderers; let us look carefully at Pojman's arguments for executing them. Those arguments fall mainly under the rubrics of desert and deterrence. I shall take these up in turn, show that they fail to establish his case, and conclude with a miscellany of other objections to Pojman's defense of the death penalty.

I. Desert, Equivalence, and Duty

Pojman argues that murderers should be executed because they deserve to die and we have a duty to give them what they deserve. These notions are in turn grounded in more general claims, namely, that evildoers deserve evil equivalent in gravity to the evil that they have done (call this *the equivalence thesis*) and that we (or our state) have a duty to give people what they deserve (call this *the duty thesis*). Unless Pojman can establish both the equivalence thesis and the duty thesis, he fails to establish that murderers should be executed because they deserve it.

Pojman begins his argument for the equivalence thesis with a series of

151

appeals to authority (13). Ancient adages, the Eastern idea of karma, words of Cicero, Leibniz, and Kant are marshaled to show the long pedigree of the idea that the good should prosper and the evil should suffer—both in equal measure to their virtue or vice. However, appeals to authority are not very persuasive. They show only that some respectable folks have held an opinion, *not* that that opinion is true. Moreover, Pojman's roster of authorities is marked by the conspicuous absence of Buddha, Socrates, and Jesus, who all taught that we should respond to evil with good.[1] And even among the authorities to whom Pojman does appeal, there is little that actually supports the equivalence thesis as such. For example, Cicero is cited for holding that justice is giving each his due. But this doesn't say what anyone's due is. And Leibniz is cited for holding that it is "morally fitting" that the evil suffer eternal damnation. Pojman thinks that "eternal hell is excessive punishment for human evil," but he asserts that Leibniz's principle of *moral fittingness* is the same principle as what Kant calls the principle of *equality*, that is, the equivalence thesis. However, when Pojman notes that eternal hell is excessive punishment for human evil, he implicitly acknowledges that Leibniz did not understand moral fittingness as equality or equivalence—eternal hell is a lot more evil than any human could have caused.

From here, Pojman turns to our primitive, spontaneous, and involuntary responses of gratitude for favors and resentment for harms. Our primitive desire "to reciprocate and harm" the one who harms us reveals to Pojman "an instinctual duty to harm" the wrongdoer. That this is instinctual to us is supported by Pojman's claim that some animals seem to respond to harm in similar ways. However, the most that an argument like this can show is that resentment and gratitude are natural to us. But our question is what is right, not what is natural. And since much that is natural (aggressiveness, dominance hierarchies, not to mention running around naked in public) needs to be limited or prohibited in light of moral

---

1. Pojman does mention Jesus here, but for commanding that we "Render unto Caesar that which is Caesar's and unto God that which is God's." This statement is about the relationship of political duties to religious duties; it says nothing about punishing or rewarding, nor about requiting good with good and evil with evil. Socrates did, to be sure, believe in punishing the evil. However, he thought that this was justified because he understood punishment as a cure for evil, and thus as benefiting the soul of the punished. See, for example, Plato's *Gorgias,* 478d-e.

considerations, what is natural cannot itself tell us what is right. Indeed, the very notion of "an instinctual duty" strikes me as incoherent. Consider that the sexual instinct is as strong as the instinct for resentment or vindication: Does it make sense to say that we have an instinctual duty to have sex? All that could be instinctive to us is a desire to act some way—be it sexually or vindictively. Perhaps we experience this instinctual desire so strongly as to make it feel like a duty. But feeling one has a duty no more entails that one really has a duty than feeling that one can fly entails that one can fly.

Moreover, while some animals may requite harm with harm, there is no evidence that they aim to requite with harm *equivalent* to what they have suffered. Thus, no support is given to the equivalence thesis even if animal behavior could give such support, which I doubt. In the treatment of our fellows, we aspire (I hope) to do better than animals. Nonetheless, Pojman moves directly from the "primordial reactions" of animals to the "primordial desert-based idea of justice," which, he says,

> has two parts. Every action in the universe has a fitting response in terms of creating a duty to punish or reward, and that response must be *appropriate* in measure to the original action. It follows that evil deeds must be followed by evil outcomes and good deeds by good outcomes, exactly equal or in proportion to the vice or virtue in question. (15)

Note that this passage affirms that evil is to be matched with evil and good with good "exactly equal *or in proportion to* the vice or virtue in question." Recall the discussion of proportional retributivism in my essay. Proportional retributivism calls for punishing criminals who do the worst crime with our worst penalty, punishing those who do the second worst crime with our second worst penalty, and so on—*without insisting on equivalence between crime and punishment*. Since, by his own statement, "appropriateness" can be satisfied with proportionate punishment that is not equivalent to the harm caused, Pojman's formulation *doesn't even assert, much less prove, the equivalence thesis*.

Regarding the duty thesis, Pojman asserts again that the evil deserve evil, that justice entails giving people what they deserve, and thus that, "[s]ince we have a general duty to strive to bring about justice in the world, it follows that we have a duty to try to bring it about . . . [that] wherever possible, the virtuous are rewarded with well-being and the vicious with suffering" (19). Suppose we grant that we have a duty to bring about justice, that justice includes people getting what they deserve, and that the evil deserve punishment and the good deserve reward. What sort of duty do we, then, have? Recall that in my essay I claimed that, while benefactors of humanity deserve rewards, no one necessarily has a duty to give them those rewards. At most, this is a weak and easily overridden duty. Now, since giving the good what they deserve is as much a part of justice as giving the evil what they deserve, our duty to punish the evil can be no stronger than our duty to reward benefactors of humanity. Then, even if we grant Pojman that there is a duty to give people what they deserve, that duty is weak and easily overridden—and thus, in effect, next to no duty at all. In fact, if this is what Pojman's view comes down to, he and I are not far apart. I share with him the belief that it is in general good to give people what they deserve; and my argument needs only the claim that we are not duty-bound to give them everything that they deserve.

Pojman writes that, "by violating the right of another to life, I thereby forfeit my right to life" (30). However, if I forfeit my right to life that means only that if someone kills me, he violates no right, maybe he does no wrong. But this doesn't imply that he has a duty to kill me, as Pojman recognizes. He continues:

> Forfeiture gives the moral and legal authority the right to inflict the criminal with a punishment, but it says nothing about the *duty* of the authority to punish. The principle of just desert completes the theory of retribution. Not only do murderers forfeit their right to life, but they positively deserve their punishment. If they have committed a capital offense, they deserve a capital punishment. If first-degree murder is on the level of the worst types of crimes, as we think it is, then we are justified in imposing the worst type of punishments on the murderer. Death would be the fitting punishment; anything less would indicate that we regarded murder a less serious offense. (30–31)

Note, first, that this passage asserts that the offender's desert implies a duty to punish him, when, as I have shown by inventorying his attempts, the most that Pojman can be said to have proven is that we have a duty here that is no stronger than the duty we have to reward humanity's benefactors. Then the passage asserts that capital criminals deserve capital punishments, when, as I have shown by inventorying his attempts, Pojman has not proven the equivalence thesis upon which this assertion is based. And the passage concludes with two sentences that imply that equivalence is not even necessary after all. Consider that the last sentence only follows from the one before it if death is our worst type of punishment. If rape or castration were our worst punishments, then it would follow that these were the fitting punishments for the murderer. And if life in prison without parole were our worst type of punishment, it would be the fitting punishment for murder. Rather than showing that death is the only fitting punishment for murder, Pojman's argument here leads to the conclusion that our worst punishment is the fitting punishment for murder—and nothing has been said to show that that must be death.

I conclude, then, that Pojman has not proven either the equivalence thesis or the duty thesis. He has not proven that justice or desert requires that we execute murderers. Nor has he proven that justice or desert cannot be satisfied with, say, life in prison without parole—legally, a "civil death"—or even with a long prison term, such as twenty years.

II. Deterrence: Common Sense and the Best Bet Argument

Pojman says of the criticism of Isaac Ehrlich's deterrence research: "One criticism . . . is that if he had omitted the years 1962 to 1969, he would have had significantly different results" (38). The criticism is far more serious than this sounds. Ehrlich studied the deterrent effect of the death penalty for the period 1933 to 1969 and found that each execution may have deterred as many as eight murders. When the period from 1963 to 1969 is eliminated, there aren't merely "different results"; rather, *no significant deterrent effect shows up at all!* But if the death penalty deters, how come this didn't show up between 1933 and 1963—particularly in view of the fact that executions were carried out very frequently in the 1930s?[2] One is almost tempted to say that Ehrlich has effectively proven that the death penalty is *not* a superior deterrent to imprisonment. But I will not argue that here.

Pojman recognizes that the empirical studies do not support a greater deterrent effect of capital punishment, but he claims that the studies are inconclusive for two reasons: first, because of the low likelihood of death

---

2. See, for example, U.S. National Criminal Justice Information and Statistics Service, *Capital Punishment 1978* (Washington, DC: Law Enforcement Assistance Administration, December 1979), 18.

penalties and, second, because of the so-called lighthouse effect (according to which, we see the cases where deterrence fails, but not those where it succeeds). Neither of these reasons is very persuasive. As to the first, death sentences were carried out quite regularly in the Depression Era, as already mentioned, and studies covering this period (even Ehrlich's!) show no increased deterrence due to capital punishment. And as to the lighthouse effect, note that the studies that show no difference in murder rates due to the death penalty compare murder rates in two jurisdictions that are similar except that one has and the other does not have the death penalty. Consequently, if the death penalty prevented murders that life imprisonment failed to prevent, this would show up in higher murder rates in the states without the death penalty. Thus this research is not subject to the lighthouse effect. My view is that the studies show no increased deterrent impact from capital punishment because there is none, for reasons that I shall suggest below.

Pojman, contending that the research has not proven that the death penalty does not deter more than life imprisonment, seeks to bolster his case by putting forth the so-called best bet argument, which he takes to be agnostic (39) on the issue of whether the death penalty is a superior deterrent to imprisonment, and he follows this argument with the commonsense argument, which purports to prove that, whatever the research shows, the death penalty is a greater deterrent after all. Since I think that the best bet argument is not really agnostic, but in fact gets some of its force from the commonsense argument, I take up the commonsense argument first.

We have already seen the commonsense argument formulated by Ernest van den Haag and Michael Davis. Pojman follows suit. The argument starts from the premise that "what people (including potential criminals) fear more will have a greater deterrent effect on them," and it goes on to say that, since people fear death more than life in prison, they "will be deterred more by the death penalty" than by other available punishments, such as life in prison (45). I have already contended, in my essay that the first premise here is a nonstarter. As David Conway pointed out, the fact that one penalty is feared more than another does not imply that the more feared penalty deters more than the less feared, since the less feared penalty may already deter me as much as I can be deterred. Says Conway,

> given the choice, I would strongly prefer one thousand years in hell to eternity there. Nonetheless, if one thousand years in hell were the penalty for

some action, it would be quite sufficient to deter me from performing that action. The additional years would do nothing to discourage me further. Similarly, the prospect of the death penalty, while worse, may not have any greater deterrent effect than does that of life imprisonment.[3]

Since this argument was made more than twenty years ago and still has not deterred van den Haag and Davis and now Pojman from using the commonsense argument, I am convinced that more must be said to show just how devastating the implications of this point are for any version of the commonsense argument. Conway's argument shows that the commonsense argument contains a questionable premise, namely, the idea that *people's disinclination to act in some way rises continuously and without limit as the fearsomeness of the penalty for that act rises.* Without this premise, the commonsense argument fails. If people's disinclination doesn't keep rising but instead tops out at some point, it is no longer possible to infer from the greater fearfulness of the death penalty its greater deterrent impact since people's disinclination may have topped out at life imprisonment. What is really devastating about Conway's point is that the continuously rising disinclination premise is part of a technical theory, and no part of common sense. Those who put forth the commonsense argument are really putting forth a theory that isn't commonsensical at all, and they're calling it common sense!

What theory is this that underlies the idea that disinclination continuously correlates with fearfulness? It is some version of psychological hedonism of the sort that one finds in textbooks of neoclassical economic theory, in which people are thought to seek continuously to maximize their net satisfaction. What we have here, then, is not the behavior of commonsense folks. It's the behavior of idealized rational consumers![4] The giveaway is Pojman's claim that criminals do cost-benefit analyses before deciding to break the law (46). Beware of equivocation here. I don't doubt that would-be criminals consider costs and benefits of potential crimes in a rough manner. I will shortly suggest a "model" of how they do so. What

---

3. See note 50 and accompanying text in my essay.
4. Michael Davis, to his credit, effectively admits this in acknowledging that his version of the commonsense argument is about *rational agents* rather than real people, and later, when he asserts that the commonsense method yields conceptual truths. But, then, it is misleading to call this common sense. Only a formalized theory of rational judgment could yield conceptual truths. See note 49 in my essay.

is highly implausible, however, is that criminals do cost-benefit analyses in the technical sense of that term, such that every increment of cost and every increment of benefit are taken into account. This is what we have to think at least a significant number of criminals are doing in order to ignore the social science findings and insist, as Pojman (and van den Haag and Davis) do, that an increase in penalty from life in prison to execution will figure in the motivation of potential murderers enough to deter additional murders. And that is simply implausible.

When John Stuart Mill tried to introduce qualitative differences in pleasures into utilitarianism, he was already responding to the implausibility of psychological hedonism understood on the model of Jeremy Bentham's calculus of pleasures and pains. (How often do you reach a decision between alternative courses of action by summing the pleasures and pains of each and following the option with the highest net sum of satisfaction? How often do you even think of pleasures as measurable and summable? Do you suppose that the pleasure of falling in love or discovering a cure for cancer is equal to the pleasure from some—even a very large—number of cheeseburgers?) If there are qualitative differences of pleasures, then it is not possible to sum up pains and pleasures and pursue maximum net satisfaction because qualitatively different pleasures are strictly incommensurable.

In any event, if there are qualitative differences in pleasures, there are surely also qualitative differences in pains and thus in fearfulness—and no longer any reason to expect that disinclination will rise continuously with fearfulness. It seems to me that this is confirmed when we observe the actual judgments and behavior of commonsensically rational people, instead of reading a theory into them. Rather than finely calibrating their reactions to increasingly negative outcomes, commonsense people seem to batch negative outcomes into qualitative groupings, such as "worth a great effort to avoid," "worth a substantial effort to avoid," and "worth only a minor effort to avoid." So being killed painfully or painlessly, being locked in prison for your whole life or for much of your life, being paralyzed, being blinded, and losing both arms or both legs are all, irrespective of their relative differences in awfulness, worth a great effort to avoid. Breaking a bone, losing a finger, getting a serious (but not permanently damaging) beating, and being injured seriously (but not gravely and permanently) in a car accident are worth a substantial effort to avoid. And getting a splinter, stubbing a toe, and falling in the street, as well as worse but very unlikely things, such as getting hit by lightening, killed in a train derailment, or contracting a rare and terrible disease, are worth only a minor effort to avoid.

I do not insist on the details of this description. I say only that it is something like what commonsensically rational people do in the face of statistically possible negative outcomes, and there's nothing irrational about it, unless one is already assuming a theory of rationality, such as that used in economics.[5] Then, when you think of potential criminals, it's only commonsensical to suppose that they do the same, treating any serious criminal penalty as "worth a great effort to avoid." I contend that the so-called cost-benefit analyses that Pojman thinks some criminals engage in amount to no finer calculation than this. And this is not only closer to the actual way in which commonsense folks treat risks, it also fits perfectly with the majority of social science studies on the death penalty, which show that the difference between life in prison and death does not alter people's inclination or disinclination to commit murder—just as if would-be murderers had batched these two penalties under one rubric and acted accordingly. I conclude that the commonsense argument for the death penalty is an impostor. It is a theory of rational behavior and not even a very plausible one. The commonsense argument fails for lack of common sense.

Pojman tries to bolster the commonsense argument with anecdotal evidence of the greater deterrent effect of capital punishment, but anecdotes are no basis upon which to justify a policy, particularly one that includes killing people. Anecdotes are afflicted with the arbitrariness of how they (rather than other stories with contrary morals) come to our attention. Moreover, anecdotes yield uncertain lessons because they rely on the judgments made by the people who figure in the anecdotes, judgments that may be false or one-sided or merely mirroring conventional and potentially

---

5. To give the economists their due, it is worth noting that the description of people's ways of dealing with statistically negative outcomes sketched here is fully compatible with the theory of rational consumer behavior when that theory is thought of as applying to very large numbers of individuals rather than as describing any particular individual's actual psychology. If people classify outcomes in the rough way I have here suggested they do, and if they choose in light of these classifications, their choices will tend to increase their satisfaction. If you plot a very large enough number of such choices, the lumpiness of each person's classification system will be averaged out by that of the others, and their choices will appear simply to follow increased net satisfaction in a smoothly incremental way.

groundless beliefs. For example, that an anecdote tells of a crook who says he stopped using a gun because the death penalty was instituted does not prove that that is the real reason why he stopped. He might, for example, have been influenced by news reports of a crackdown on crime, or by a television show about criminals getting caught, or by a dozen other influences that may work on his mind without his full awareness of their impact. It is precisely because of these limitations on the truth content of anecdotes that we have recourse to the more controlled methods of social science. To use anecdotes to improve on social science is like going to a shaman because you don't like what your doctor has told you.

I turn now to the best bet argument. The best bet argument holds that, because execution *might* deter murderers, it is better to execute murderers than not to. Executing murderers may deter someone from killing an innocent person, and if not, all we have lost is one dead murderer. Not executing may have no impact on future criminals, but if there are any who would have been deterred by execution, then we have failed to stop the killing of an innocent person. Since it seems worse to fail to stop the killing of the innocent than to kill a murderer without a deterrent gain, our best bet is to execute murderers.

I put off dealing with the best bet argument until now because that argument looks very weak without the commonsense argument accompanying it. For unless there is some reason to expect the death penalty to be a superior deterrent to life in prison, the best bet argument calls for the merest toying with human beings, which seems offensive even when the human beings are murderers. It is one thing to kill murderers when there is reason to think it will protect innocents, but to kill them because of the bare possibility that this might happen seems like exactly the kind of disrespectful treatment of the murderer that Kant condemned. So, without either a showing from social science or from common sense that the death penalty is likely to save lives, I think the best bet argument fails.

Some people may resist this conclusion, holding that, since murderers are of less worth than innocent people (Pojman puts their comparative value at 1 to 1,000 [41]), the bare possibility that executing a murderer might save an innocent is enough to justify the death penalty as our best bet. There is, I think, a further argument against this approach that I think refutes it finally. Recall that in my essay, I argued that, by refraining from executing murderers, the state will contribute to the general repugnance of murder, and I speculated that *this will lead to fewer murders over time.*

Moreover, there is a line of social science research defending the so-called brutalization hypothesis, which purports to show that murders increase in the period following executions and that these are real increases (not just changes in timing).[6] If either or both of these claims are plausible, then the outcomes facing us in the best bet argument are dramatically changed. Now, in addition to no evidence that the death penalty deters more murders, there is the additional possibility that the death penalty increases the number of murders. Then, there is no reason to bet on executions over life imprisonment in the name of future innocent victims. Executions may protect them or jeopardize them. With that, the best bet argument evaporates.

III. Concluding Miscellany

Pojman repeats van den Haag's argument against the claim that the biased way in which the death penalty is administered disqualifies it as a legitimate punishment policy. Pojman argues that that is a problem with the application of the penalty, not with the death penalty itself (56). And he repeats van den Haag's argument against the claim that poverty is a cause of crime. Pojman points out that crime rates in absolutely poorer countries are often lower than ours (3). In my essay, I showed that the first of these van den Haagian arguments saves the justice of the death penalty *in principle* at the price of leaving standing the argument against instituting it *in practice* and that the second of these van den Haagian arguments rests on an oversimplified reading of the claim about poverty and crime (119, 127–28).

More important, Pojman thinks he has gotten rid of the bias argument in pointing out that a slightly higher percentage of whites arrested for murder are executed than the percentage of blacks arrested for murder who get executed (58n72). He ignores the presence of racist bias in arrest practices[7] and the well-documented bias in the imposition of the death

---

6. See note 54 and accompanying text in my essay.

7. For example, in 1993, respondents to the Department of Justice's National Criminal Victimization Survey reported that 32 percent of their assailants in violent victimizations (rape, robbery, and aggravated assault) were perceived to be black, whereas 45 percent of those arrested for rape, robbery, and aggravated assault that year were black (U.S. Department of Justice, Bureau of Justice Statistics, *Sourcebook of Criminal Justice Statistics, 1994*, ed. Kathleen Maguire and Ann L. Pastore [Washington, DC: U.S. Government Printing Office, 1995], Table 3.28, p. 243; Table 4.11, p. 388).

penalty by race of the victim and the way in which this bias undermines the state's moral authority to impose the death penalty.[8] Moreover, this evidence of racist bias comes after the Supreme Court threw out death penalty statutes in 1972 (because of arbitrariness and discrimination) and then allowed new death penalty statutes in 1976 (held to have removed the main sources of arbitrariness and discrimination).[9] In short, the bias occurred *after* the system was reformed, suggesting that the problem runs too deep to be corrected by reform. Finally, Pojman does accept that there is economic bias against the poor in the imposition of capital punishment (58n72), and that is equally undermining of the state's moral authority to impose the penalty.

Pojman puts forth something that he calls "the Golden Rule argument for the death penalty" (51). Instead of an argument, however, one finds a series of rhetorical questions, such as "if you had kidnapped a young girl, placed her in your trunk, and then killed her, what punishment do you think would be fitting for *you*?," which Pojman assumes his readers will answer in ways that show their agreement on the rightness of capital punishment. Note, first of all, that this has little to do with the Golden Rule, which asks you to treat people as you would want to be treated by them, and thus at most asks, "If you did some awful crime, how would you *want* to be treated?"—a question to which most folks would probably answer, "with mercy." Kant regarded the Golden Rule as of limited worth, in part because "the criminal would on this ground be able to dispute with the judges who punish him."[10] Further, Pojman ought to pose his questions to a thoughtful objector to the death penalty. I suspect that Pojman would not get the answers he expects. And that should be enough to show that he has put forth as an argument what is no more than a set of intuitions, his own, coupled with the unverified assumption that others will share them and that they are probative—neither of which seems to be the case.

Finally, Pojman contends that those opponents of capital punishment who support a woman's right to abortion—such as Supreme Court Justice William Brennan—are inconsistent in allowing the killing of fetuses who

---

8. See notes 77 and 78 and accompanying text in my essay.

9. *Furman v Georgia*, 408 US 238 (1972); and *Gregg v Georgia*, 428 US 153 (1976).

10. Immanuel Kant, *Grounding for the Metaphysics of Morals*, trans. J. W. Ellington (Indianapolis, IN: Hackett Publishing, 1981; originally published 1785), 37n.

are "innocent of any wrongdoing" but opposing the killing of murderers who "deserve death" (63). As applied to Brennan, the charge is way off-base, inasmuch as he was not rendering moral decisions, but determining what the U.S. Constitution requires. However, even as moral decisions, there is no inconsistency here whatsoever. Pojman acknowledges that those in the pro-choice camp hold that "fetuses are not *persons.*"[11] Having recognized this, Pojman goes on, without argument, to affirm in effect that a fetus is morally comparable to an adult human being because the "fetus progressively nears personhood." One might just as well argue that a long fly ball that goes foul only by inches ought to get some of the credit given to a home run because it's so close. However near to personhood it may be, a fetus is not yet a person. What Pojman fails to see is that, here, as in baseball, a miss is as good as a mile. Not being a person, a fetus does not yet have a person's right to life, and thus a fetus is morally incomparable to a murderer, who (whatever else he is) is a person. There is no more inconsistency in saying that it is wrong to kill (guilty) persons but okay to kill (innocent) nonpersons than it would be to say that it is wrong to kill (guilty) murderers but okay to kill (innocent) animals.

---

11. See, for example, Michael Tooley, *Abortion and Infanticide* (Oxford: Clarendon Press, 1983); Mary Anne Warren, "On the Moral and Legal Status of Abortion," in *The Problem of Abortion*, 2nd ed., ed. Joel Feinberg (Belmont, CA: Wadsworth Publishing, 1984), 110–14; S. I. Benn, "Abortion, Infanticide, and Respect for Persons," in *Problem of Abortion*, ed. Feinberg, 135–144; Jeffrey Reiman, "Abortion, Infanticide, and the Asymmetric Value of Human Life," in *Journal of Social Philosophy* 27, no. 3 (Winter 1996): 181–200; and Jeffrey Reiman, *Critical Moral Liberalism: Theory and Practice* (Lanham, MD: Rowman & Littlefield, 1997), 189–210.

Index

abortion, 6, 63–64, 143, 144, 162–63
accidental injury, 89n28. *See also* automobile accidents
accountability. *See* responsibility
African Americans. *See* black persons
afterlife, 114n66, 136; Conway on, 104n50, 140n3, 156–57; Leibniz on, 13–14, 152
alcoholic beverages, 30n32
Alfred P. Murrah Federal Building, 4, 51
American Bar Association, 118, 126n86, 146–47, 148
American Journal of Public Health, 124
American Medical Association, 147
American Revolution, 108n57
amnesia, 33–34
Amnesty International, 144
anecdotal evidence, 38–39, 44–51, 65, 102–7, 156–60
anesthetics, 108n57, 145
angioplasty, 141
animals, 35; conflicts among, 2; evolution from, 36; killing of, 144, 163; reactions of, 15, 152; requital by, 153
appeals process, 54, 62, 129
Arab-Israel War (1967), 6
Ariès, Philippe, 114n66
Arizona, 148, 149
arrest practices, 161

asbestos, 124
Asians, 148
assaulters, 107, 112, 161n7
Auerbach, Paul, 1–2
Australia, 2n3
Austria, 2, 32, 58n73, 62
automobile accidents, 13, 54. *See also* vehicular homicide
automobile driving right, 30n32
automobile insurance, 42
automobile tire spikes, 80, 82
autonomy, 25, 142. *See also* responsibility

Baldus, David, 38, 122n77
Bangladesh, 2
bank presidents, 32n34
Barshay, Hyman, 46–47
Barzun, Jacques, 55
Beccaria, Cesare de, 29
Bedau, Hugo Adam: on abolishment, 50; on dead victims, 51; on deterrence, 100–101; on equivalences, 93; on juries, 114n65; on miscarriages of justice, 53–54; on punishment limits, 94; on retributivism, 72n8; on social objectives, 58–59
benefactors, 87, 136, 138–39, 154
Benn, Stanley I., 12–13, 22, 23, 88n27
Bentham, Jeremy, 22, 158

165

About the Authors

Louis Paul Pojman grew up in Cicero, Illinois. He attended New Bruns-wick Theological Seminary before becoming a minister of a black church in Bedford-Stuyvesant, Brooklyn in the 1960s. He was a civil rights activ-ist, leading integration projects and participating in demonstrations. In 1969 he was a Fulbright Fellow at the University of Copenhagen, and in 1970 he was a Rockefeller Fellow at Hamburg University. He received his Ph.D. in philosophy from Oxford University in 1977. He has taught at the University of Notre Dame, the University of Texas at Dallas and the University of Mississippi before coming to the United States Military Academy at West Point.

Louis Pojman is the author or editor of over twenty books and seventy-five articles. He has won several research and teaching awards, including the Burlington Northern Award for Outstanding Teaching and Scholar-ship (1988) and the Outstanding Scholar/Teacher in the Humanities at the University of Mississippi (1994). He and his wife are avid hikers and environmentalists. He is a vegetarian, a bicyclist and a member of Amnesty International.

Jeffrey Reiman is William Fraser McDowell Professor of Philosophy at American University in Washington, D.C. Born in Brooklyn, New York, in 1942, Reiman received his B.A. in philosophy from Queens College in 1963 and his Ph.D. in philosophy from Pennsylvania State University in 1968. He was a Fulbright Scholar in India during 1966–67.

Reiman joined the American University faculty in 1970 in the Center for the Administration of Justice (now called the Department of Justice, Law and Society of the School of Public Affairs). After several years of holding a joint appointment in the Justice program and the Department of Philosophy and Religion, he joined the Department of Philosophy and Religion full-time in 1988, becoming director of the Master's Program in

Philosophy and Social Policy. He was named William Fraser McDowell Professor of Philosophy in 1990.

Reiman is a member of the Phi Beta Kappa and Phi Kappa Phi honor societies and president of the American University Phi Beta Kappa chapter. He is the author of *In Defense of Political Philosophy* (Harper & Row, 1972), *Justice and Modern Moral Philosophy* (Yale University Press, 1990), *Critical Moral Liberalism: Theory and Practice* (Rowman & Littlefield, 1997), and *The Rich Get Richer and the Poor Get Prison: Ideology, Class, and Criminal Justice* (5th edition, Allyn & Bacon, 1998), and more than fifty articles in philosophy and criminal justice journals and anthologies.